Therapeutic Groups for Obese Women

D1362601

Therapeutic Groups for Obese Women

A Group Leader's Handbook

Julia Buckroyd and Sharon Rother

Obesity and Eating Disorders Research Unit, Health and Human Research Institute, University of Hertfordshire, UK

BICENTENNIAL
1807
WILEY
2007
BICENTENNIAL

John Wiley & Sons, Ltd

Copyright © 2007   John Wiley & Sons Ltd, The Atrium, Southern Gate, Chichester,
West Sussex PO19 8SQ, England

Telephone (+44) 1243 779777

Email (for orders and customer service enquiries): cs-books@wiley.co.uk
Visit our Home Page on www.wiley.com

All Rights Reserved. No part of this publication may be reproduced, stored in a retrieval system or transmitted in any form or by any means, electronic, mechanical, photocopying, recording, scanning or otherwise, except under the terms of the Copyright, Designs and Patents Act 1988 or under the terms of a licence issued by the Copyright Licensing Agency Ltd, 90 Tottenham Court Road, London W1T 4LP, UK, without the permission in writing of the Publisher. Requests to the Publisher should be addressed to the Permissions Department, John Wiley & Sons Ltd, The Atrium, Southern Gate, Chichester, West Sussex PO19 8SQ, England, or emailed to permreq@wiley.co.uk, or faxed to (+44) 1243 770620.

Designations used by companies to distinguish their products are often claimed as trademarks. All brand names and product names used in this book are trade names, service marks, trademarks or registered trademarks of their respective owners. The Publisher is not associated with any product or vendor mentioned in this book.

This publication is designed to provide accurate and authoritative information in regard to the subject matter covered. It is sold on the understanding that the Publisher is not engaged in rendering professional services. If professional advice or other expert assistance is required, the services of a competent professional should be sought.

Other Wiley Editorial Offices

John Wiley & Sons Inc., 111 River Street, Hoboken, NJ 07030, USA

Jossey-Bass, 989 Market Street, San Francisco, CA 94103-1741, USA

Wiley-VCH Verlag GmbH, Boschstr. 12, D-69469 Weinheim, Germany

John Wiley & Sons Australia Ltd, 42 McDougall Street, Milton, Queensland 4064, Australia

John Wiley & Sons (Asia) Pte Ltd, 2 Clementi Loop #02-01, Jin Xing Distripark, Singapore 129809

John Wiley & Sons Canada Ltd, 6045 Freemont Blvd, Mississauga, ONT, L5R 4J3

Wiley also publishes its books in a variety of electronic formats. Some content that appears in print may not be available in electronic books.

Anniversary Logo Design: Richard J. Pacifico

Library of Congress Cataloging-in-Publication Data

Buckroyd, Julia.
 Therapeutic groups for obese women : a group leader's handbook / Julia Buckroyd and Sharon Rother.
  p. ; cm.
 Includes bibliographical references and index.
 ISBN 978-0-470-03448-4 (pbk. : alk. paper)
1. Obesity–Treatment. 2. Obesity in women–Treatment. 3. Group psychotherapy. I. Rother, Sharon. II. Title.
 [DNLM: 1. Obesity–therapy. 2. Cognitive Therapy–methods. 3. Psychotherapy, Group–methods. 4. Women–psychology. WD 210 B925t 2007]
 RC628.B83 2007
 362.196'3980082–dc22

                                                                2007002344

British Library Cataloguing in Publication Data

A catalogue record for this book is available from the British Library

ISBN 978-0-470-03448-4 (pbk)

Typeset in 11/13 pt Times by Thomson Digital, India
Printed and bound in Great Britain by Antony Rowe, Chippenham, Wiltshire
This book is printed on acid-free paper responsibly manufactured from sustainable forestry
in which at least two trees are planted for each one used for paper production.

Contents

About the Authors   ix

Preface   xi

Acknowledgements   xiii

Introduction   xv

PART I: BACKGROUND   1

Chapter 1: Guiding Principles   3

Chapter 2: Transtheoretical Elements of the Treatment   9

Chapter 3: Constituent Parts of the Treatment   15

Chapter 4: Description of the Research Programme   33

Chapter 5: Experience of Running the Treatment Groups   37

Chapter 6: Training for Leading a Treatment Group   49

PART II: THE PROGRAMME   51

Introduction to the Programme   52

Session 1   53

Session 2   57

Session 3   61

Session 4   65

Session 5   69

Session 6   73

Session 7   79

Session 8   83

Contents

Session 9   87

Session 10   89

Session 11   93

Session 12   97

Session 13   101

Session 14   105

Session 15   107

Session 16   111

Session 17   113

Session 18   117

Session 19   119

Session 20   121

Session 21   123

Session 22   125

Session 23   127

Session 24   129

Session 25   133

Session 26   135

Session 27   139

Session 28   141

Session 29   143

Session 30   145

Session 31   147

Session 32   149

Contents

Session 33   151

Session 34   153

Session 35   155

Session 36   157

PART III: APPENDICES   **161**

Appendix 1: Group confidentiality statement   163

Appendix 2: Outline of the Programme   165

Appendix 3: Process of Change   167

Appendix 4: Food and Mood Sheet   169

Appendix 5: How a Child Learns to Manage Feelings   171

Appendix 6: Meal Planner   173

Appendix 7: Questions for 'Food in the Family' Exercise   175

Appendix 8: Overview of First 12 Weeks   177

Appendix 9: Guided Fantasy   179

Appendix 10: Overview of First 24 Weeks   181

Appendix 11: Overview of Entire 36 Weeks   183

References   187

Index   203

About the Authors

Julia Buckroyd is Professor of Counselling at the University of Hertfordshire and Director of the Obesity and Eating Disorders Research Unit. She trained first as a counsellor and then as a psychotherapist and has worked clinically in the field of eating disorders since 1984. Her interest in obesity grew out of her work with eating disordered young women and she has brought to it many of the psychological perspectives current in that field. She began carrying out research into the treatment of obesity in 1999 and has developed an ongoing portfolio of research projects. She can be contacted at j.buckroyd@herts.ac.uk.

Sharon Rother is a Lecturer in Counselling and Research Coordinator for the Obesity and Eating Disorders Research Unit at the University of Hertfordshire. She completed an MA in Counselling Inquiry for which she investigated recovery in anorexics. She trained as a counsellor and currently continues a practice, specialising in working with eating-disordered and obese people. She has worked in the field of obesity research with Julia Buckroyd since 2002, and can be contacted at s.m.rother@herts.ac.uk.

Preface

We are sure we are not alone as health professionals in our experience of the difficulty in helping obese people lose weight. Permanent weight loss has been impossible to achieve for about 80% of overweight people, yet the serious consequences of being very overweight are well documented. The obese women with whom we have worked have tried repeatedly, but without success, to lose weight and keep it off; by the time they come to us they are desperate. The response to them, which this book describes, has evolved over about eight years and is built on our work as therapists with women with disordered eating. It will not be suitable for all those who want to lose weight. We present, in the first part of what follows, our argument for thinking that within the total group of obese people there is a subgroup of perhaps 30–50% whose eating is driven by emotional issues and who have a background of psychological distress. It is for the women in this group that our programme has evolved.

In what follows we discuss the research literature that has brought us to these conclusions and consider how this group of patients can be identified. We describe how the research literature has influenced the shape and content of the intervention and its five themes. We discuss the context of the research we are undertaking in which the programme evolved, and share with readers our experience of running the groups. We also discuss the skills that will be required of those who wish to conduct the programme. We then present the programme in detail week by week over 36 sessions. Ample freedom is given to the group leader to modify the pace of the programme according to her clinical judgement. Illustrative examples are provided of responses to the various elements of the programme.

Although we are in the process of testing the programme we do not yet have results to demonstrate its effectiveness. We offer it to health professionals on the basis that it has been devised in accordance with the research literature and offers an innovative approach to a patient group whose needs are plainly not being met by current interventions. We are committed to the publication of results as they become available and would also welcome feedback from those who make use of the programme.

Julia Buckroyd
Sharon Rother
November 2006

The workbook appendices included in this book are available online, free to purchasers of the print version. Visit the website www.wiley.com/go/obesity to find out how to access and download this material.

Acknowledgements

Our programme has evolved over the last eight years. During that time we have been indebted to many people who have helped us in different ways.

The preliminary work was carried out with support from the European Social Fund and the University of Hertfordshire. The current project, testing the programme presented here, has been funded by the Hertfordshire Primary Care Research Network (HertNet), Dacorum Primary Care Trust and the University of Hertfordshire RAE Capability Funding.

The University of Hertfordshire has been consistently helpful and supportive of the work. We are particularly grateful to our Head of Department, Dr Michael Buckenham, for his sustained belief in our research.

We have been involved with a good number of voluntary sector counselling agencies within Hertfordshire who have facilitated the development of our work by sharing their experience of working with very overweight women, by generously allowing us to use their premises and by referring their clients to us.

The research programme has benefited from collaboration with a substantial number of NHS Health Professionals. We would particularly like to mention Kay Shrimpton in Stevenage, Gill Goodlad in Hemel Hempstead, Jane Hamill in Welwyn, Diana Foley in Hitchin and Claire Foley in Welwyn Garden City.

We owe a particular debt of gratitude to our group leaders who embarked on a journey of training and group leadership that lasted several years and shared with us what they learned as the project continued. They are Marian Brindle, Carol Bush, Linda Eke, Joan Irvine and Diane Redfern. We are also grateful to colleagues, research students and research assistants who engaged with us in many discussions of the issues raised in the book and whose work has informed our writing. In particular we would like to thank Sarah Barnett, Jacqueline Bidgood, Patricia Goodspeed-Grant, George Green, Colleen Heenan, Jenny Mirani, Barbara Scott, Deborah Seamoore, Nel Walker and Sue Williams.

Most of all we are grateful to our participants who share so much with us and trust us to do our best to help them.

Introduction

The work described in this book addresses the relatively new and very serious problem of obesity and describes an integrated group treatment for obese women designed to effect maintained weight loss. As is well known, rates of obesity have increased very significantly over the past 20 years and continue to escalate (WHO, 1997). In 1980 6% of men and 8% of women were classified as obese in the UK. By 2002 the proportions had increased to 23% of men and 25% of women (House of Commons Health Committee, 2004; Rennie & Jebb, 2005). The health risks (Conway & Rene, 2004) and the many other social, psychological and economic consequences that result from obesity have become a major cause of concern, especially in developed economies (Field et al., 2002; Wolf, 2002; Haslam & James, 2005).

The implications of obesity for the national economy and the health of the nation have led to the issuing of government advice in relation to what is seen as a developing crisis in the UK. This advice has been, and continues to be, heavily dominated by the conventional recommendations to eat less and exercise more (DOH, 2004). NIHCE guidelines published in December 2006 constitute largely advice to improve food choice, reduce the amount eaten and increase activity. Where these initiatives fail, drug treatments and stomach surgery are recommended. Similar authoritative advice from the US Department of Health and Human Services (National Institutes of Health, 2000) gives 10 steps to treating obesity in the primary care setting. These 10 steps emphasise dietary restriction and physical activity, yet make no mention whatever of psychological factors.

Yet, as early as 1991, Garner and Wooley were reporting 'overwhelming evidence that [behavioral and dietary treatments of obesity] are ineffective in producing lasting weight loss' (p. 729). This reality has been obscured because almost everybody can secure short-term weight loss via dietary restriction (Garner & Wooley, 1991). Disappointingly, 'short-term results are frankly misleading indicators of long-term outcome' (p. 737). They reported abundant evidence 'that most individuals will regain most or all of their weight after four or five years' (p. 736). As they comment, dietary restriction maintained by willpower is simply too difficult for most people. A substantial minority of obese people, perhaps 20–30% of those seeking treatment, suffer from binge eating disorder (BED) (Devlin et al., 1992). Both cognitive behavioural therapy (CBT) and inter-personal therapy (IPT) have resulted in a reduction in bingeing but, unfortunately, neither these treatments nor behavioural weight loss treatment for BED have been shown to produce maintained weight loss (Wilson et al., 2000). Devlin (2001) is similarly convinced that 'sustained weight loss [for patients presenting with both obesity and BED] remains a largely unrealised goal'. Glenny and O'Meara (1997) reviewed the prevention and treatment of obesity and concluded that although a number of treatments had been shown to achieve weight loss, weight regain was common and modified only by long-term follow-up strategies. Douketis et al. (1999) reviewed material on the detection, prevention and treatment of obesity and concluded that there was a lack of evidence supporting the long-term effectiveness of weight reduction methods. Harvey et al. (2002) reviewed health professionals' management of obesity and concluded that 'at present there are few solid leads about improving obesity management'.

It seems clear that so far all attempts at treatment, with the possible exception of the very drastic solution of surgery, are ineffective in producing maintained weight loss (Garner & Wooley, 1991; Cogan & Ernsberger, 1999; Jeffery et al., 2000; Haslam & James, 2005). Surgery may also be a problematic solution because of its cost and the need for continuing monitoring for side effects. A recent sustained follow-up indicates a complication rate of almost 40% (Encinosa, 2006). Pharmaceutical remedies such as Orlistat (Sjöström et al., 1998), Sibutramine (James et al., 2000) and Rimonabant (Van Gaal et al., 2005; Despré et al., 2005) are likely to be imperfect long-term solutions with all the dangers of the side effects of long-term pharmacotherapy and the typical weight regain when medication is withdrawn (Perri, 1998; Collins & Williams, 2001; O'Meara et al., 2001, 2004). In fact, treatment has proved such a challenge that recent researchers have proposed that obesity be accepted as a chronic disease in order to focus greater resources on its treatment (NHLBI, 1998; Perri, 1998; Liebbrand & Fichter, 2002; Conway & Rene, 2004).

However, we continue to be interested in the problem of effecting maintained weight loss so that our focus over the past seven years has been in developing a treatment for those who are already obese. Our work so far has been exclusively with women. It remains to be seen whether the approach we describe is also appropriate for men.

Before we go any further and start to describe the treatment we have developed, we would like to raise the issue of whether our treatment is suitable for all obese women. There are currently approximately 15 million obese people in the UK. To date, treatments that have been developed have been assumed to be equally suitable for all obese people. Those who have sought to understand why only a small percentage of participants in the treatments maintain a clinically significant weight loss have generally provided the very frustrating answer that the people who are successful are those who maintain a pattern of careful eating, attention to their weight and regular exercise (Pronk & Wing, 1994; Klem et al., 1997; Wing & Klem, 2002). Unfortunately, this is an entirely circular argument, since what we need to know is not how to maintain weight loss in a practical way, but how to enable people to follow these precepts; as Byrne et al. (2004) comment, 'relapse appears to be attributable to the individual's inability to persist with the behavioural strategies needed to maintain the new lower weight' (p. 1341).

As Foster and Kendall (1994) and Wilson (1994) both suggest, it is unlikely that all obese people are the same, psychologically speaking, or that all obese people will respond to a single approach. Foster and Kendall identify 'the psychological heterogeneity of obese persons' (p. 711) and suggest that 'a significant percentage of obese patients, presenting for treatment, may require psychotherapy or pharmacotherapy in addition to any obesity treatment' (p. 711). Although differences have been identified for some considerable time and the need for differential treatments understood (Brownell & Wadden, 1992; Schwartz & Brownell, 1995) no progress has so far been made in matching treatments to individual needs.

An early paper by Colvin and Olson (1983) identified autonomy, or a recognition of responsibility, as a relevant feature of those who maintain weight loss. Recent work by Texeira et al. (2005) takes up this theme. They attempted to discover whether it was possible to predict treatment outcomes by identifying significant predictors of weight loss. They identified that treatment meant a reduced calorie diet, sometimes with exercise, and a behaviour modification component. They discovered that the people who benefited from this treatment were those who had few previous weight loss attempts (as Jeffery et al., 1984 had previously found) and an autonomous, self-motivated, cognitive style. Our understanding of this work is that Texeira et al. have demonstrated that a specific treatment (reduced calorie, exercise + behaviour modification) works for a specific group of people (few previous weight loss attempts and an autonomous, self-motivated, cognitive style).

But the women we have worked with have been dramatically different from those that Texeira et al. describe. They have been binge eaters and emotional eaters; they have had difficult histories and now often live in difficult circumstances; and they have had multiple experiences of weight loss and regain. We would like to propose that the treatment we have developed is suitable for those women but very unlikely to be suitable for those that Texeira et al. describe. We see the intervention, described in this book, as not simply facilitating changes in eating behaviour, and therefore weight, but also addressing psychological issues and offering a programme of lifestyle change which also addresses food use and activity.

As psychological therapists we have extrapolated from our work with eating-disordered women the idea that disordered eating of whatever kind is, at least in part, driven by psychological issues. Whereas the treatment of eating disorders has moved steadily away from an exclusive focus on eating behaviour, the treatment of obesity is characteristically entirely focused on eating behaviour. Building on the work of feminist psychotherapists and, more recently, cognitive behavioural therapists, we have developed a group treatment that not only incorporates attention to food choices and activity levels but also makes use of the considerable body of evidence that links psychological issues and eating behaviour.

The fundamental hypothesis on which the work is based is that eating behaviour for all human beings is affected by social, psychological and cultural factors (Ogden, 2003; Logue, 2004). In particular we believe that the eating behaviour of many people is influenced by psychological factors, particularly those to do with the regulation of affect. We have found, in a process of continuing informal enquiry, that women, of whatever weight, readily accept the proposition that their eating behaviour is affected by their mood and, moreover, will spontaneously supply us with examples. We have often heard how eating is affected by boredom, frustration, depression, etc. We also notice that our language encapsulates this behaviour in the phrase 'comfort eating'. We further hypothesise that the degree to which emotional eating is employed varies greatly within the population and that those who employ it to a greater extent are likely to be more overweight. This relationship has not yet been formally tested but we are in the process of carrying out studies that will begin to explore that relationship.

We are not proposing that all obesity can be accounted for in this way. There is a wide range of physiological and biochemical mechanisms that affect appetite and eating behaviour (accessibly reviewed in Logue, 2004). Other factors such as the decline in activity, the greater availability of food, the popularity of calorie-dense food and changes in social structures around eating are likely to be involved. Genetic inheritance certainly also plays a part (Chagnon et al., 2003) but perhaps not as great a part as some would argue (Collins & Williams, 2001) as does socio-economic status (Parsons et al., 1999; Leather, 2003). Nevertheless, it seems plain to us that changing eating behaviour, for many people, is a psychologically and emotionally more complex task than has so far been recognised.

The whole of the treatment programme described in this book is based on the premise that obesity, for a significant proportion of people, is strongly associated with psychological issues. The research that we are about to describe can so far only suggest how many obese people may be responding with their eating behaviour to psychological issues but proposes a profile of the kind of person who may be suitable for our programme.

Our hypothesis, at its widest, is that food is used by many obese people as a way of managing their emotional lives. We suspect that obesity coincides, not only with a toxic environment of abundant, available, inexpensive, calorie-dense food, but also with the breakdown of the fabric of society which has previously sustained and contained people in the UK. This factor is probably true for numbers of other societies and it may be that the western cultures that suffer most from obesity (notably the USA) are also those where social disintegration is most obvious (Kasser, 2002; James, 2007). Some authors have carried out research that supports our ideas about the breakdown of social support and have shown that the fragmentation of family and community support systems has health effects and may increase the number of those using food for 'comfort' (Egolf et al., 1992; Forbes, 1994; McElroy, 2002).

We believe that people need each other to manage life events and circumstances that affect us all. Historically the need for emotional support has been met by families and by the plethora of social and community associations, which include religious groups, youth groups, uniformed organisations and community groups. Currently this social support has fragmented. It seems to us that people are unsupported in a way that is new and that alternative social groupings are slow to develop.

We suspect that in this vacuum many people look for other means of managing day to day. We notice the enormous increase in every addictive and compulsive activity you can name (Orford, 2001). We consider that overeating is one of these activities, less harmful than many others and more available than most (and affecting about one-quarter of the UK population). We believe that the general failure of exhortations to eat less and exercise more becomes intelligible if we understand that excessive consumption can have meaning and, indeed, is a necessary part of some people's way of managing their lives.

It stands to reason that giving up one's way of coping will not be sustained in the long run unless some alternative has been developed. Our programme seeks to help participants to identify the meaning of their overeating and to develop alternative strategies, particularly better relationships, to cope with whatever life brings them.

In support of this hypothesis, we would like to present some of the research literature, which leads us to think that for substantial numbers of obese people a consideration of psychological factors is highly relevant.

Eating disorders research (as opposed to obesity research) has repeatedly shown that there is a high probability that the over-consumption or restriction of food is an emotionally driven activity. In fact a number of authors suggest that it is normative for food to be used in all human societies for other than physiological purposes (Ogden, 1998, 2000, 2003; Canetti et al., 2002; Logue, 2004). Ogden, in particular, has shown the enormous complexity of the way that food is used by all of us, including those who are in no way 'eating disordered'. Hayward et al. (2000) agree that 'complex health problems [such as obesity] are replete with social and psychological factors that may undermine treatment success. Understanding a client's experience while attempting behavior change is crucial for the development of interventions that address difficult and costly health behaviors' (p. 616). Life events and their emotional consequences often result in abnormal food use in the wider population (Rookus et al., 1988). It may not, therefore, be very surprising to think that obesity for some people may be the result of an emotional use of food.

Some attempt has been made to identify abnormal eating patterns both in the general population and in the obese population. Binge eating has been extensively studied, especially in relation to aversive emotional states (Heatherton & Baumeister, 1991; Kenardy et al., 1996; Telch & Agras, 1996; Vogele & Florin, 1997; Deaver et al., 2003; Chua et al., 2004). Marcus and Wing (1987) found that between 20% and 46% of obese individuals in a weight control programme reported binge eating (see also Yanovski, 2003a). More recently Gluck et al. (2004) reported that up to 46% of those defined as obese do in fact binge eat, and binge eating appears to be more common in females (Freeman & Gil, 2004; Linde et al., 2004). On the basis of this evidence it looks as though almost half of all obese people may be using food to manage difficult feelings. Foreyt and Goodrick (1994) found that weight regain was associated, among other things, with life stress, negative coping style and emotional or binge-eating patterns. Fichter et al. (1993) and Agras et al. (1997) reported that binge eating predicted weight regain.

Canetti et al. (2002) looked at the relationship between emotions and food intake, and concluded that, in particular, negative emotions, increase food consumption among normal weight people as well as overweight people. They also concluded that the influence of emotions on eating behaviour is stronger in obese people and confirmed that obese people eat in response to emotions more than normal weight people. Benjamin and Kamin-Shaaltiel (2004), for instance, related overweight in Israeli women to anger avoidance. We suppose that they imply that food is used to enable the suppression or management of anger.

Steptoe et al. (1998) determined that stress leading to increased distress stimulated alterations in food choice towards greater intake of fat and sugar, in vulnerable individuals. Popkess-Vawter et al. (1998) identified power/control, relationships with others and unpleasant feelings as triggers for overeating in overweight women. Epel et al. (2001) show that artificially induced stress promotes 'comfort food intake'. Schoemaker et al. (2002) and Freeman and Gil (2004) report that stress precipitates binge eating. Rosmond (2005) is also interested in the relationship between stress and visceral obesity, and suggests that persistent stress results in the release of excess cortisol which, in turn, promotes visceral obesity. Gluck et al. (2004) came to the same conclusion. Conversely, Heinrichs et al. (2003) discovered that social support and oxytocin suppressed cortisol production.

Geliebter and Aversa (2003) reported that overweight individuals overate during negative emotional states and situations. Byrne et al. (2003) identified the use of eating to regulate mood, or to distract from unpleasant thoughts and moods, as one characteristic of obese women who had lost a substantial amount of weight and then regained it. Walfish (2004) found that 40% of a sample of bariatric surgery patients could be identified as 'emotional eaters' and recommended treatment to address this problem to increase the likelihood of long-term maintenance of weight loss.

There is substantial evidence to suggest that those who use food for affect regulation may have significant psychological issues relating to their history. Attachment history has been studied extensively for its relationship to affect regulation. Schore has developed a clear model for the relationship between attachment history, its neurological consequences and the person's capacity to regulate affect. 'Enduring structural changes [as a result of traumatic attachments] lead to the inefficient stress coping mechanisms that lie at the core of . . . post traumatic stress disorders' (Schore, 2002, p. 11; see also Raynes et al., 1989; Zimmerman, 1999; Schore, 2000, 2001, 2003). A review of attachment research in eating disorders (Ward et al., 2000) concluded that insecure attachment is common in eating-disordered populations. Maunder and Hunter (2001) have extended the scope of the enquiry to evaluate the evidence linking attachment insecurity to illness generally. They cautiously proposed that overeating, leading to obesity, may be a means of managing insecure attachment. Flores (2001) related attachment difficulties to addiction and substance abuse as a means of self-repair. Trombini et al. (2003) found that obese children and their mothers had a significant prevalence of insecure attachment style and recommended that treatment of obesity in children needed to include a psychological intervention with the mother. Vila et al. (2004) similarly identified disturbance in the families of obese children and recommended family treatment. Ciechanowski et al. (2004) found that avoidant attachment patterns were associated with poorer self-management in patients with diabetes – there is an 85% association of Type 2 diabetes and obesity (Eberhardt et al., 2004). Troisi et al. (2005) commented that 'persons with eating disorders are expected to have a high frequency of adverse early experiences with their attachment figures and a high prevalence of insecure attachment . . .. The insecure attachment style has been also considered as a risk factor for the development of an eating disorder' (p. 89). Tasca et al. (2006) reported that both attachment anxiety and attachment avoidance were related to poorer outcomes in group treatment for binge eating disorder.

Attachment difficulties may well be associated with difficult early experiences (Prior & Glaser, 2006). Felitti (one of the first researchers to explore these themes) observed a 55% dropout rate in a weight loss programme despite the fact that dropouts had been losing weight, not gaining. This observation and subsequent interviews and studies (Felitti, 1991, 1993) indicated that overeating and obesity were often unconscious 'protective solutions to unrecognised problems dating back to childhood' (Felitti, 2003, p. 2).

Felitti's work stimulated an epidemiological study in collaboration with researchers from the Center for Disease Control and Prevention (CDC) in Atlanta, USA: the 'Adverse Childhood Experiences (ACE) Study'. This study sought to examine the relationship between childhood abuse and family dysfunction and many of the leading causes of adult mortality (Felitti et al., 1998). Eight categories of experiences (ACEs) that could adversely affect a child were developed, three of which were direct actions: physical, verbal and sexual abuse. The other five addressed environmentally adverse experiences such as loss, neglect or trauma; violence against mother; growing up in a household with members who had been imprisoned, were substance abusers, or who were depressed, suicidal or had untreated mental illness. Of 17,337 adult participants more than 50% reported at least one ACE, and 25% reported at least two. Those that reported four or more ACEs were at increased risk for substance abuse (drugs, alcohol, smoking), mental health problems, cancer, heart disease, chronic pulmonary disease, etc. In relation to obesity, the study found that people who had experienced four or more ACEs had a 1.4 to 1.6-fold increased risk for severe obesity and inactivity (Felitti et al., 1998).

A number of other authors have explored the relationship between earlier adverse life experiences, eating disorders and obesity (Kopp, 1994; Lissau & Sotrensen, 1994; Kent et al., 1999; Williamson et al., 2001; Wonderlich et al., 2001) In a review of the literature of childhood sexual abuse (CSA) and obesity, Gustafson and Sarwer (2004) note that 'studies suggest at least a modest relationship between the two'. A similar result was found in a review by Smolak and Murnen (2002) who found that CSA is associated with an increased likelihood of eating disorder symptoms. A positive correlation between CSA and binge eating has been found (Grilo & Masheb, 2001; Wonderlich et al., 2001). It is possible that binge eating is the mediating factor between CSA and obesity.

Mills (1995) found that adults whose obesity dated from childhood had poorer mental health than those who became obese later in life, suggesting early traumatic experience. Power and Parsons (2000) suggested that emotional deprivation in childhood might be related to adult obesity. In studies by Grilo and colleagues, 83% of participants with binge eating disorder reported some form of childhood maltreatment (Grilo & Masheb, 2001). (BED is a diagnostic description of bingeing combined with a loss of a sense of control that occurs twice a week or more over a period of six months.) A study of bariatric (stomach) surgery patients found that half the females had experienced early sexual abuse (Rowston et al., 1992) and abuse history was significantly related to overweight/obesity in a sample of female gastrointestinal patients (Jia et al., 2004). In a study of extremely obese bariatric surgery candidates, 69% reported maltreatment (Grilo et al., 2005).

Longitudinal studies, over a period of seven years, of sexually abused children revealed higher rates of healthcare utilization and long-term health problems than comparison groups, and both studies mention comparatively higher rates of overweight and obesity in the abused groups (Frothingham et al., 2000; Sickel et al., 2002). While there are few long-term studies, there is varied literature on the effects of early abuse and neglect upon adult health

(Roberts, 1996; Weiss et al., 1999; Stein & Barret-Connor, 2000; MacMillan et al., 2001, Kendall-Tackett, 2002; Hulme, 2004; Leserman, 2005) and there is some evidence that CSA may negatively influence weight loss in obesity treatment (King et al., 1996). Wiederman et al. (1999) discuss how obesity may have an adaptive function for sexually abused women, which lends some support to the findings of Felitti (1993) where participants reported using obesity as a sexually protective device, and overeating to manage emotional distress.

Much of the data quoted above has been gathered by means of questionnaires. However, when obese people have been given the opportunity to talk about their obesity at greater length, the findings have shown very similar results. Qualitative studies have consistently demonstrated the association of poor family functioning and excess use of food. These studies have also shown the importance of the social environment and food use in response to negative affect. Stress, anxiety and loneliness are particularly identified in the data (Lyons, 1998; Sarlio-Lahteenkorva, 1998; Bidgood & Buckroyd, 2005; Davis et al., 2005; Goodspeed-Grant & Boersma, 2005). Work that we have recently carried out again confirms these findings (Buckroyd et al. in preparation c). A sample of 79 obese women seeking treatment were asked at first interview what factors they thought were involved in their obesity. As expected many practical factors were identified, including bad diet, overeating, etc., but all of them also attributed their eating behaviour to emotional factors. These mainly ranged from particular feeling states, e.g. boredom, depression, anxiety, to current life events, e.g. relationship problems, bereavement, illness, etc., to reports of adverse childhood experiences.

If psychological factors and obesity can be linked, as the above evidence suggests, we need to know precisely how they may be linked. In the past ten years or so evidence has been accumulating which suggests that eating particular comfort foods – foods high in fat and carbohydrate – has an effect on the biochemistry of the brain which reduce stress or produces hedonic effects (Colantuoni et al., 2002; Will et al., 2003, 2004). Yanovski (2003b) found that the opioid system might be involved in response to ingestion of sweet, high-fat foods by women. Lowe and Levine (2005) have proposed that the presence of highly palatable food is enough to activate a hedonic appetite system. Apparently the prospect of the pleasurable results of eating is a powerful force. Dallman et al. (2005) demonstrate that eating comfort foods reduces the effects of chronic stress by modifying the biochemical effects. She urges that, rather than accepting that those in chronic stress will indulge in comfort foods and thus become obese, the chronic stressor should be removed. She proposes, therefore, that obesity might be less common 'were policy makers aware of the insidious effects of not actively seeking to relieve sources of uncontrollable chronic stressors' (p. 279). This is a long way from urging obese people to eat less.

This data does not demonstrate that all obese people use food for emotional purposes. It does, however, show that the emotional use of food is normative in the non-obese population and that a significant proportion, perhaps approaching 50% of obese people, seem to use food to manage their emotional lives to such an extent that they become obese. Our programme, therefore, proceeds on the assumption that sustained weight loss will not be achieved for these people unless such emotional issues are addressed and alternative coping strategies are adopted.

The question remains: How can that proportion of obese people to whom these issues are relevant be identified or, in other words, how can we match individuals to the treatment we are offering? At the moment there is no good answer to this question, identified by Rössner, Brownell and Wadden as early as 1992, reiterated by Schwartz and Brownell in 1995 and also thought important by Jeffery et al. (2000). However, it seems likely that those who score highly on measures of binge eating and emotional eating are likely to fall into this category. As Felitti remarked in 2003, the use of food to manage psychological issues may be unconscious, and responses to questionnaires on emotional eating will therefore be unreliable. Nevertheless there seems to be a strong correlation between emotional eating and binge eating (Eldredge & Agras, 1996; Telch & Agras, 1996), so that binge eating may be a useful proxy measure.

Elfhag et al. (2003) have also been concerned to identify subgroups among the populaton of obese people. She thought that two subgroups could be identified: one characterised by difficulties with emotions, binge eating and experiencing body size as having psychological meaning. This sounds very much like the group we have been working with. The other group was characterised by coping liabilities, a lower socio-economic level and irregular or chaotic meal patterns. She suggests that this second group might need to find a structure for eating and lifestyle changes. It may well be that these two groups overlap to some extent, but the treatment for those who need a structure for eating and lifestyle changes might well be a shorter and more practical behaviour modification treatment than the programme we are proposing. It is possible that those who benefit from commercial weight loss programmes may do so because of the structures that are imposed by them.

Our conclusion is, therefore, that we seek to identify a subgroup among treatment-seeking obese women who acknowledge binge eating and are receptive to the idea that their eating behaviour may be influenced by their emotions.

Research on psychological treatments for obesity

In 2004 Hay et al. carried out a Cochrane Review on psychotherapy for bulimia nervosa and bingeing, which concluded that there was some support for the use of CBT but that these treatments did not contribute to weight loss. Another recent Cochrane Review by Shaw et al. (2005) assessed the effects of psychological interventions for overweight or obesity as a means of achieving sustained weight loss. They concluded that psychological interventions, particularly behavioural and cognitive behavioural strategies, enhance weight reduction and that they are predominantly useful when combined with dietary and exercise strategies. They commented that other psychological interventions have been less rigorously evaluated for their efficacy as weight loss treatments. Unfortunately this review comments principally on weight loss. For inclusion, follow-up was required for only three months, and few studies were long term. As the authors comment, without longer term studies the true effect of psychological interventions on weight is difficult to determine.

This authoritative review therefore takes us very little further forward in identifying an appropriate psychological treatment for maintained weight loss. Although we are currently researching our own treatment we are certainly not in a position to assure you that we can solve this very difficult problem. However, we consider that the evidence we have quoted above of the importance of psychological issues to a significant proportion of obese people, supports our fundamental hypothesis of the need to address the psychological issues.

Before proceeding we would like to give a brief outline of the intervention, which is described in much greater detail in the rest of this book.

A group of approximately 10 women, conforming to the psychological profile identified above, with a BMI $\geq$ 35 is recruited to meet on a weekly basis for two hours for 36 sessions (Body Mass Index (BMI) is calculated by dividing weight in kilograms by height in metres squared). It is likely that these 36 sessions will be spread over a calendar year once holidays have been included. The intervention is led by a group leader who has trained as a psychological therapist and has undertaken additional training in running a group of this kind. The principal objective of the group is to enable maintained weight loss $\geq$ 5–10% of baseline weight for two years. The intervention is structured in three 12 week 'terms'. The first term addresses the psychological meaning of food and eating behaviour to individual members. It also provides cognitive behavioural strategies for modifying eating behaviour. The second term continues these themes and adds the subject of food choice which is similarly addressed from a psychotherapeutic and cognitive behavioural perspective. The third term continues these three themes while adding attention to increased activity. Activity is also addressed from a psychotherapeutic and cognitive behavioural perspective.

PART I
Background

Chapter 1
Guiding Principles

Introduction

Psychological treatments of whatever kind are based on differing theories and understandings of human development and functioning and incorporate value systems that focus on different aspects of human behaviour. Our judgement is that these theories often privilege the understanding of one aspect of human behaviour over others so, for example, person-centred theory has privileged feelings, psychodynamic theory has privileged insight, cognitive behavioural theory has privileged thinking, behavioural theory has privileged behaviour. In what follows we have described briefly the range of theories and accompanying value systems that we have found useful. We have also provided a short account of the particular relevance of these theories to our client group of obese women. We do not pretend to have developed a comprehensive account of human functioning, rather our understanding has been pragmatically driven to use what works. We have also been influenced by recent research that seems to demonstrate fairly conclusively what has come to be known as the 'dodo' effect (reviewed usefully by O'Brien & Houston, 2000). The 'dodo' effect supports the idea that what works in therapy is not the particular modality in which it is delivered (e.g. psychodynamic, CBT) but characteristics that are transmodal. These appear to focus on 'the ability to engage the client in a cooperative participation with regard to the goals and tasks of therapy, to provide an opportunity for the client to express emotion and to create a healing, therapeutic bond' (O'Brien & Houston, 2000, p. 37). In our discussion of the conduct of the group and the training of the group leaders these transmodal elements are stressed.

We are also aware of research which suggests that there are different learning styles. These seem to correspond to people who learn more easily from words as opposed to those who learn more easily from diagrams and illustrations and, secondly, to those who have a grasp of a whole subject as opposed to those who focus on the detail of a part of a subject (Riding & Rayner, 1998). The integration of different modalities in our programme may give room for these differences. We have tried to use a combination of verbal and visual activities although the weight of the programme is certainly towards the verbal.

Similarly we have tried to provide a balance between the detail of individual sessions and activities and a picture of the whole. Each session begins with its overview and a recapitulation of the previous session. At the beginning of the programme we provide an overview of the whole programme (Appendix 2). Similarly at the end of each 12 week block there is the opportunity for review and an overview.

It may be that different clients make use of some elements of our programme more than others. We are hoping to provide a range of ways of understanding eating behaviour so that the participants in our groups can make use of those elements that have most resonance for them. Much of the language of different theories is metaphorical. It may be that, in time, neuroscience (Schore, 1997a, 1997b, 1997c, 2000, 2002, 2003) will be able to help us to understand more exactly how different interventions impact on the brain and inform our choices so that psychotherapy of all kinds can be delivered more effectively. In the meantime we are offering a buffet.

In what follows we describe the range of theories we have employed. They are all based on the assumption that human beings are capable of emotional growth and development; as the British Association for Counselling and Psychotherapy says 'Counselling is a way of enabling choice or change or of reducing confusion' (www.bacp.co.uk/education/whatiscounselling.html).

Carl Rogers and Person centred theory

We have been concerned in carrying out our research and in developing the programme, to ensure that our participants are treated with respect and empathy. This may seem a self-evident principle for working with patients of any kind. However the literature reveals, and the evidence provided by our participants confirms, that respect and empathy cannot be assumed in the treatment of obese people.

Discrimination against obese people is common (Garner & Wooley, 1991; Fabricatore & Wadden, 2004) and has been identified in areas including employment, housing and healthcare (Friedman & Brownell, 2002; Harvey et al., 2002b). Puhl and Brownell (2002) describe discrimination in employment, healthcare and education. A study by Carryer (2001) describes the experience of nine 'large bodied women' which reports discrimination by nurses and suggests strategies for improving their responses to large women. Obese people themselves report significant difficulty in continuing a normal social life and find themselves discriminated against in both work and social situations (Crisp, 1988; Lee & Shapiro, 2003). Women in particular are stigmatised for being obese (Rothblum, 1994; Cogan & Ernsberger, 1999). One study confirmed widespread prejudice against overweight women when eating out (Zdrodowski, 1996).

Our own research has supported the findings that obese people experience prejudice and discrimination. In a study conducted with a community sample of obese people, participants were explicit about the prejudice they encountered:

> People, if you're fat, don't take you seriously and they don't have much respect for you either.
> I don't like going out. I like to sit at home . . . because I know people talk about me behind my back.
> If you're waiting to be served, you can be overlooked. . . big as you are, you can be invisible. People make snide comments to each other in lifts. In passing they will stare.

[People] seem to think you're fair game to be treated like garbage and talked to like rubbish–you don't have feelings. I may be very big on the outside, but on the inside I've got the feelings of a size 10 and if anything I'm as fragile, if not more fragile.

(Bidgood & Buckroyd, 2005, p. 224)

The participants in our study encountered prejudice and stigmatisation in a wide range of situations: in shops, restaurants, places of entertainment and recreation, public transport, and even in hospitals in one case. Apparently the National Health Service wheelchair is not strong enough for anyone weighing more than 22 stone/140 kilograms (White, 2002). Participants felt that the needs of large people are ignored: seats on buses, coaches and aircraft were too narrow, seatbelts were almost impossible to use. Job prospects for the participants were diminished, for men as well as women, due to the difficulty of overcoming the immediate hurdle of gaining acceptance into the job in the first place. In many cases such widespread prejudice and stigmatisation had resulted in the participants withdrawing from social life and hiding away at home as much as possible (Bidgood & Buckroyd, 2005). A Cochrane Review (Harvey et al., 2002b) on improving health professionals' management and the organisation of care for overweight and obese people concluded, rather depressingly, that there was little to suggest how the management of obesity might be improved.

Our recognition of all the deeply felt hurt that results from this prejudice and stigmatisation has made us determined to offer a different environment in which to work with our participants. We have taken Carl Rogers (1979, 1981) and, more recently, Tudor et al. (2004) as valuable guides to placing the women we work with at the centre of our concern. Rogers' supreme insight, explored in many different ways in his published work, was that change is more likely to take place in an environment of safety and respect. He codified this understanding in what he called the 'core conditions'. These include congruence, empathy and unconditional positive regard. When troubled people are met with these conditions they tend to be able to resolve their difficulties and embark on a process of change. Rogers believed that given this facilitating environment, the inherent capacity for change in positive directions that all of us possess, can be activated. This theory fits in well with the research on transmodal counselling described above (O'Brien & Houston, 2000).

Psychodynamic theory

This basic framework of respect for our participants is amplified by psychodynamic ideas, that is to say, those ideas that derive from Freud and his successors over the past hundred years. We have both trained extensively as psychodynamic practitioners and, although we have both since developed an integrative approach to our therapeutic work, we make use of a good many psychodynamic ideas. Most basic of these is the idea that symptoms (in this case obesity) have meaning. Our fundamental understanding of obesity in the subgroup of obese people that we have identified is that it results from eating behaviour that is, in part, emotionally driven. We regard the symptom (i.e. the eating behaviour and resultant obesity) as evidence of emotional distress. In other words, we believe that obesity is not simply the result of a poor diet or a lack of exercise, but has emotional meaning.

A second fundamental psychodynamic idea that is important to our work is the conviction that the past has a powerful effect on the present and that many of our habits of all kinds are formed by early experience. To this basic understanding we add a particular respect for attachment theory (Sroufe, 1995; Bowlby, 2000a, 2000b, 2000c; Stern, 2000; Holmes, 2003; Howe, 2003). We consider that attachment theory, one of the best evidenced elements of modern psychodynamic theory, is extremely helpful in describing the patterns of relationship which derive from the past and get re-enacted in the present. It has been our clinical experience that coming to a better awareness of the influence of the past on the present can be a huge relief to our participants. An initial suspicion, voiced by most of our participants that their eating behaviour is influenced by feelings and life events, is developed so that their behaviour becomes more meaningful to them. They can then often stop describing themselves as greedy or lacking willpower, for example, and acknowledge that their eating and their obesity make sense (Buckroyd et al., 2006). When they are less hostile to themselves they have more space in which to make choices about their behaviour.

We also make use of the psychodynamic understanding of an inner self which is composed of different 'voices' or parts. It seems helpful to think that the different parts of the self (popularised, for example, in phrases such as 'the inner child') are in relationship with each other and that at different times one or other part of the self may be more powerful or influential (Summers, 1994). Again it has been our experience that to talk in metaphors of this kind can be helpful, especially to women who find self-care difficult. The idea of the development of an internal good mother, for example, can often help them to offer support to parts of themselves that would otherwise seek solace in food.

A related area of psychodynamic thinking that we have found particularly helpful is the work of Heinz Kohut (Kohut, 1984; Siegel, 1996; Mollon, 2001; Lessem, 2005). Kohut was interested in the development of the self and in the conditions necessary to create a strong sense of self in the child and young person. He is sometimes seen as a theorist who bridges psychoanalytic and person-centred theory (Kahn 1997). He believes that conditions rather similar to those that Rogers describes as the Core Conditions, develop a robust sense of self. Since our participants uniformly demonstrate very poor self-esteem we have been influenced by Kohut's ideas of how this early damage can be repaired in a therapeutic relationship. So, for example, we have emphasised the acknowledgement of participants' strengths and successes and recognised that they need to experience the group leader as a positive figure who acknowledges their feelings and their struggle.

Feminist theory

Issues concerning eating behaviour and body esteem have, at least in the past, been seen to concern women far more than men. (Currently, in the UK, rates of obesity for men lag only a couple of percentage points behind those for women). Feminist writers have interested themselves in providing an account of women's relationships with their bodies and with food in a patriarchal society (e.g. Orbach, 1978; Lawrence & Dana, 1990; Polivy & Herman, 1992; Burgard & Lyons, 1994; Fallon et al., 1994; Bloom et al., 1999; Heenan, 2005). Our experience of working with women suffering from eating disorders, and with obese women, has not persuaded us that the feminist account of these issues is to be preferred above other accounts. We do think their contribution is valuable for some women but not meaningful for all.

However, there are aspects of feminist theory that we have adopted. One important element derives from the feminist conviction that the personal is political. It is common in therapeutic circles for distress to be seen entirely as the product of the individual's experience. Feminists have been as interested in how the culture limits and shapes women's experience, and consequently their behaviour. Among our participants, for example, there was great reluctance to engage in exercise or swimming in a mixed sex environment. The women felt unwilling to be subject to the gaze of men. An uninformed observer might accuse them of being unwilling to exercise and, therefore, failing to take responsibility for their own health but, from a feminist perspective, the culture deprives them of that freedom (McElroy, 2002). We have tried to listen carefully to our participants' experience of their own environment and to be attentive to their needs from that perspective. We have, for example, run the groups in term time, recognising that otherwise childcare obligations would prevent some of our participants from attending.

A second aspect of feminist practice that we have adopted has been to diminish the power differential between group leader and participant as far possible. The hierarchies of a patriarchal society are the common experience of women, especially those from a deprived background. We seek to provide a different experience. We have done this by seeking opportunities to empower our participants to devise their own remedies. So, for example, we have not drafted in 'expert' nutritionists or dieticians or exercise specialists (as is commonly done in weight maintenance groups) because our experience has been that our group members have, between them, a vast store of latent knowledge of these issues. They do not need an expert to tell them what to do; they need encouragement to make active what they already know. Similarly, the group leader we see as providing the facilitating environment for the group to work rather than functioning as the expert. Our image is of collaboration.

Cognitive behavioural therapy

Cognitive behavioural therapy (CBT) is an exceedingly well-known therapy that has demonstrated its value via research much more than most other methods. It is based on the premise that we all view our current experience through the prism of the past. In our formative years we develop beliefs as a result of our experience and we continue to act on those beliefs whether or not they are appropriate in the light of current experience. So, the person who has learned that no one will be interested in her distress as a child and that food is a more reliable comforter, will tend to act on this belief even if her experience of people in the present does not reflect her earlier experience.

It is the task of the CBT practitioner to engage the client in a series of 'experiments' to find out whether her thinking is accurate or not. It is a therapy that has little interest in the past or how clients may have arrived at the convictions they hold but instead it focuses on changing those convictions in the present. Common faults in thinking such as all or nothing thinking (I've eaten a cream bun and spoiled my diet so I may as well eat 10 cream buns) or catastrophising (I've eaten a cream bun so I'm never going to lose any weight) can be challenged and explored using CBT. For that reason it has been widely adopted for many different client populations, including obese people. Shaw et al. (2005) reviewed CBT as an adjunct to dietary and exercise strategies for achieving weight loss but unfortunately were not able to comment on its value for achieving maintained weight loss.

Cooper et al. (2003) have published a CBT programme for obese people in individual treatment. This programme begins with a conventional calorie-counting, food-restricting diet programme based on a daily intake of 1,500 calories. It is followed by close attention to problems in keeping to this diet and encouragement to increase activity using largely behavioural strategies. Attention is focused on challenging failure to conform to the programme's requirements. Recommendations for healthy eating are included. The second phase of the programme addresses obstacles to maintaining weight loss, including improving body image using cognitive strategies. Patients are supported to pursue their life goals whether or not they have lost weight. The authors stress the value of the final phase of the programme, which teaches strategies for monitoring weight, anticipating problems in maintaining their diet programme and developing a personal weight maintenance plan. Although the authors are researching the long-term effectiveness of their plan for weight loss maintenance, results were not available at the time of writing. However, the programme incorporates areas of functioning that have been demonstrated to be involved in the process of weight loss and weight loss maintenance. These include a reduction in calorific intake and increase in activity, attention to body esteem, strategies for managing situations likely to trigger overeating and, most particularly, attention to ways of thinking that undermine the patients' belief in their capacity for maintained weight loss.

We have also used many of the above strategies to engage our participants' cognitive strengths to support the emotional growth that we are trying to encourage in our groups. So, for example, when we explore the emotions associated with eating particular foods and the memories these foods evoke, we then invite participants to consider whether they need to continue with the patterns they have carried over from the past. We also challenge participants' convictions that they, for example, cannot plan their eating, cannot choose healthy food and cannot find strategies to manage situations such as eating out. Most fundamentally, we challenge their conviction, born of repeated weight loss and regain, that they are unable to achieve the changes in their lives that will enable them to maintain weight loss.

We have been influenced by Yalom's belief that a cognitive structure is desirable as part of a group therapy (Yalom, 2005). For this reason we have provided an overview of the intervention to be given to participants in the first session, as well as opportunities for review after each 12-week section. We have adopted CBT strategies of homework setting and have also provided throughout, a rationale for the activities in the group, although this has not necessarily been provided first. Sometimes we have wanted the group members to experience something emotionally before we talked about it.

Chapter 2
Transtheoretical Elements of the Treatment

Introduction

In running our groups we wanted to take advantage of work in other disciplines which has focused on the psychology of change and development and of eating behaviour. We are of course fundamentally interested in behaviour change although we focus more than most on understanding psychological and emotional aspects of behaviour. We found Conner and Armitage (2002) and Ogden (2003) particularly useful in guiding us through a literature in social and health psychology that was relatively new to us.

Three contributions to social and health psychology have informed our work. The first is the theory of change developed over many years by Prochaska and DiClemente, the second is the theory of self-efficacy developed by Bandura, and the third is the theory of the value of groups, developed by numerous authors. We are especially interested in those whose work relates to therapeutic groups and social support.

Theory of change

Prochaska and DiClemente have spent their working lives creating models of the process of change (1984). The version of their work that we have used is represented in Figure 2.1, although it can also be represented on a line or a spiral.

Its strengths for the purposes of our groups seem to be as follows. Firstly, it shows change as a process with different stages taking place over a period of time. Our personal experience, and certainly the experience of our participants, is that change is a difficult or even impossible challenge. It seems that their expectation is that they can move from one set of behaviours to another without difficulty, while at the same time their experience is that after a very short time any change will be reversed. For many of them this has created an unwillingness to attempt any change. For example, many of our participants say that they will never diet again because they have had such a lot of experience of failure. The idea of a process gives them more hope.

Secondly, the figure includes and normalises the idea of relapse. The idea of relapse as part of the process of change helps to dispel the fantasy that change can or should be something achieved without hesitation or interruption. It also allows for the resumption of the process of change after relapse and so modifies the tendency to think that failure means that there is no point in continuing to attempt change.

Thirdly, the figure enables us, as facilitators, to invite group members to identify for themselves where they are in relation to any aspect of the programme. So, for instance, when we

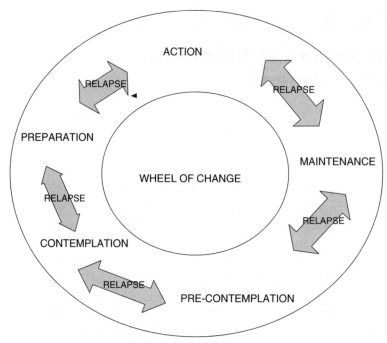

Figure 2.1   The Wheel of Change. (Adapted from Prochaska and DiClemente, 1984)

introduce the notion of increased activity, we invite the group to identify where they are in the process of change in relation to increasing activity. This enables us to see whether additional work needs to be done to prepare the participants for action before the step counters are handed out, so that we increase the likelihood that they will be used, and used constructively.

Fourthly, the use of Figure 2.1 places the responsibility for the change process firmly at the door of the participant. By identifying where they are in the change process, the group members implicitly acknowledge their own responsibility for change. By this means the group leader minimises the likelihood that she will be seen as requiring, or imposing, change and so lessens the chance that the group members will see change as her project and not theirs. Other researchers (Rothman et al., 1993) have found that taking responsibility for health promoting behaviour results in behaviour change for women accessing mammography. A similar attribution of responsibility is likely to help women to change their eating behaviour.

Prochaska et al. (1992, 1993) found that using the change model, and tailoring treatment to the individual's stage on it, vastly improved success rates for smoking cessation and was relevant to the treatment of addictive behaviours. Logue et al. (2000) recommended the use of the model to allow primary care professionals to identify when obese patients might be receptive to treatment. Kasila et al. (2003) used the model to identify patients' readiness for dietary change. They found that understanding where the patients were in relation to the change process enabled health professionals to empower patients and to modify professional interventions to each individual.

Self-efficacy

Albert Bandura is a social psychologist who has developed the idea that a person's capacity to carry out tasks, and particularly those relating to change, is directly related to a belief that they will be successful. This he calls self-efficacy (Bandura, 1997). This quality has been shown to be of relevance in weight control. Bandura reviews research literature which demonstrates the value of self-efficacy in the regulation of eating and exercise habits and concludes 'that perceived efficacy predicts weight management at each phase of change in eating and exercise habits' (1997, p. 351). Lewis et al. (1992) used self-efficacy among other strategies in a group therapy for sustained weight loss. Schwarzer and Fuchs (1995) consider that 'self-efficacy [for weight control] operates best in concert with general lifestyle changes, including physical exercise and provision of social support. Self-confident clients of intervention programs were less likely to relapse to their previous unhealthful diet' (p. 266). Goodrick et al. (1999) found that increases in eating self-efficacy were associated with reductions in binge eating severity. Conversely, low self-efficacy has been associated by a number of authors with weight regain (Gormally et al. 1980; Colvin & Olson, 1983; Jeffery et al., 1984; Tinker & Tucker, 1997). Since our programme aims at lifestyle change and provides the social support of the group it has seemed especially appropriate to incorporate the ideas of self-efficacy.

Bandura recommends that self-efficacy can be strengthened via a number of routes (1997). The first is 'mastery experiences', that is to say, the more experience people have of success the more they believe they can succeed. Considerable effort is expended during our programme both in setting achievable goals and in developing participants' strategies to succeed in reaching these goals. Secondly, Bandura believes that social modelling is important in strengthening a sense of self-efficacy. The group provides a ready made set of social models who are struggling with very similar problems and whose sharing of successes and failures is very important to individual participants. The group leader is also available to teach skills and strategies for behaviour change. Thirdly, Bandura believes in the importance of social persuasion. The positive and supportive tone of the group process contributes to this end. Finally, Bandura believes that improved emotional and physical functioning enhances self-efficacy. Group leaders consistently affirm progress and encourage further effort in these directions.

Groups

The number of obese people in developed societies seems likely to overwhelm healthcare systems. Finding a response that is effective and affordable will be a major challenge in the next two decades. It is to be hoped that prevention work, in its many developing forms, will ensure that the number of people who become obese is much reduced. There is some moderately encouraging data when very far-reaching public health initiatives are established, as they have been in Finland (Puska et al., 1985). Unfortunately it seems unlikely that a society such as the UK would support initiatives of that kind. It seems improbable that changes on a large scale will happen quickly, especially if our growing conviction – that food (among other activities and substances) is used to manage the social disintegration within western society – is correct. We believe that the health decrements of obesity will demand initiatives to deal with obese people, particularly very obese people. It seems obvious that if group treatment can work as well or better than individual treatment, then it should be adopted.

The research has not yet been carried out that would enable a comparison of these two modes of treatment although most weight loss treatment is carried out in group settings (Hayaki & Brownell 1996; Renjilian et al., 2001). Cognolato et al. (1996) reported good results from a psychodynamic group with obese patients but the numbers were very small and the results cannot be more than suggestive. More useful results are reported by McKisack and Waller (1997) who investigated factors influencing the outcome of group psychotherapy for bulimia nervosa. They found that there was no evidence to suggest an advantage to any single therapeutic orientation but that better outcomes were associated with longer, more intensively scheduled, groups and with the addition of other treatment components. They also reported that relatively larger groups were a viable option (although the largest was only nine participants).

Conviction of the value of group treatment for obesity therefore rests largely on the evidence for the generic value of groups. This is not the place to argue for the effectiveness of groups. However, group leaders need to bear in mind that, although the programme is semi-structured and involves the leader in taking an active role, the ordinary features of group functioning and development will still apply. We recommend Yalom (2005), Benson (2001) and Aveline and Dryden (1988) for helpful information.

There are a number of characteristics of group functioning that we would like to point out will be of particular relevance to the client group concerned. Firstly, we would like to discuss those to do with stages of the group process. Group process involves a number of stages differently labelled by different theorists (e.g. Tuckman, 1965; Garland et al., 1965; Hartford, 1972; Schutz, 1979). We have used a four-stage model: an initial stage when the group is formed; a stage when rivalries and anxieties predominate; a stage when the group coheres and works to achieve its objectives; and an ending stage. These stages need particular thought in reference to groups of obese women:

- Group therapy, especially in the initial stage, involves a tension between the wish to be an individual and the wish to be one of a group. Our experience is that obese women who conform to the subgroup we have described, have a powerful urge to remain separate rather than to become involved with others. There is a significant danger that the group will never form or that some members will feel unable to join and will drop out in the early sessions. The task of the group leader, to make the group a safe enough place for long-standing methods of self-reliance to be laid aside, is particularly difficult with this patient group. The homogeneous nature of the group may assist in this task; members may recognise that others have similar problems and experiences.
- The second stage involves the expression of difficult feelings. Research on alexithymia, (p. 16) demonstrates that it is very common for obese women to have difficulty in identifying, let alone expressing, feelings of anger, discontent, dissatisfaction, etc. Indeed, their use of food may well be directed to keeping them distracted from these feelings. There is a danger then, that dissatisfied group members will drop out because they have no means of negotiating difficult feelings. Alternatively they may turn the group into something bland, so that the feelings cannot be

expressed. In the first 12 weeks of the group a good deal of work is done on naming feelings to develop this skill, but the group leader needs to bear these considerations in mind and facilitate the expression of awkward feelings to the best of her ability. Emotional competence of this kind is known to be related to well-being (Ciarrochi & Scott, 2006).

- The third stage involves the emotional involvement of the group members with each other. This is of particular significance to obese women who, as research shows, are characteristically socially and emotionally isolated and have poor relationships. It is particularly important that the bonds between group members at this stage of the group are supported and encouraged so that they build an experience of mutual help and support.

- The final stage of the group involves an end of relationships that have almost certainly been important to the members. The hope is that the learning in the group will transfer to situations in relationships in ordinary life. The programme for this group emphasises the issue of relationships throughout, precisely because this is such an area of difficulty for obese women. The task of the group leader in the ending stage is to ensure as best she can that the ending is not seen as yet another disappointing failure of attachment.

There are also a number of issues for the group leader to keep in mind in relation to her task:

- The group leader in this model of group work needs to be able to assume authority. This is not a group in which the leader is the passive observer of the group process. By definition, obese women manage their emotional lives with food rather than with people. Group members need to see modelled, by the group leader, patterns of interaction and response. The group leader is the one who has a vision of how emotions can be managed with the help of other people. The group members are most unlikely to have that vision and depend on the group leader to facilitate its realisation in the group. They need to see her naming feelings and demonstrating her competence in containing and discussing them. The group also needs to see that the leader responds empathically to attempts at communication of feelings, whether positive or negative, and no matter how clumsily expressed, in order to have the courage to attempt communication themselves.

- In an active group of this kind a tension can develop between the need to attend to the task as laid out in the programme and the need to attend to the group process. The advantage of a programme is that it aims at specific outcomes and provides a focus for the work. It also creates a structure and a procedure for helping the group achieve its objectives (Benson, 2001). However, unless the leader ensures that the group members are able to work together, it will be impossible to carry out the programme. On the other hand, this is not a classic group therapy where the task is almost exclusively to attend to relationships between the members, and where the learning is focused on becoming aware of how group members interrelate. Modes of relating will, in any case, become obvious as the tasks are carried out. It will be a matter of judgement for the group leader to determine how much attention is paid to these dynamics.

Chapter 3
Constituent Parts of the Treatment

In this part of the book we first of all describe the aims and objectives of the programme. We then go on to describe the central themes of the programme and the ways they are implemented within the programme.

Aims and objectives

Aims

- If the data on the effects of obesity on physical and emotional well-being is taken at all seriously it seems evident that sustained weight loss $\geq$ 5–10% of baseline weight, is the crucial result which will deliver significant benefits (Blackburn, 2002; Seidell & Tijhuis, 2002). The first aim is, therefore, to offer a lifestyle change programme which will have this result, via investigation of the meaning of eating behaviour; strategies for improving eating behaviour; improved food choice and increased activity. This will be measured by recording BMI at base line, 12 weeks, 36 weeks, 36 weeks + six months and 36 weeks + two years.
- The second aim is to effect a general improvement in the health of participants as a result of weight loss and increased activity, which is assessed via the proxy measure of blood pressure. Blood pressure is measured at the same intervals as BMI.
- The third aim is to improve the eating behaviour of participants so that they reduce the amount of emotional eating and binge eating both of which are known to contribute to obesity. These changes are measured at the same intervals as weight and blood pressure using the Binge Eating Scale (Gormally et al., 1982) and the Emotional Eating Scale (Arnow et al., 1995).
- The fourth aim is to offer a programme of counselling in a supportive group environment which addresses psychological problems that are contributing to inappropriate eating behaviour but which also manifest as emotional distress. Changes in this area are evaluated via a measure of emotional health such as Clinical Outcomes in Routine Evaluations (CORE) (Evans et al., 2000).

Subsidiary aims

- Because obesity is closely related to food choice, emotional meanings of inappropriate food choices are explored and cognitive strategies for their improvement are offered.
- Weight maintenance is known to be associated with minimum levels of activity. The programme reviews emotional meanings of activity and offers cognitive and behavioural strategies for the improvement of levels of activity using stepometers.

Objectives

- Weight loss $\geq$ 5–10 % of baseline weight sustained for two years post-intervention.
- Stabilisation of blood pressure within the normal range.
- Reduction of emotional eating as measured by the Emotional Eating Scale (Arnow et al., 1995).
- Reduction of binge eating as measured by the Binge Eating Scale (Gormally et al., 1982).
- Improvement of the emotional well-being of the participants as measured by CORE (Evans et al., 2000).

Subsidiary objectives

- Improvement of food choice towards a standard appropriate diet, as reported by participants.
- Improvement in activity levels as measured by stepometers and reported by participants.

As you read through the programme you will have to decide how much outcome measurement you want to include. The judgement you make may well relate to the specifics of your client group and the circumstances in which the group is conducted. We recommend at least an audit of participants. We would be interested in creating a central data pool of any results you may gather. Contact us at the University of Hertfordshire: j.buckroyd@herts.ac.uk, or s.m.rother@herts.ac.uk

The five major themes of the programme are described below. The first three themes-developing emotional intelligence, developing the capacity for self nurture and developing relationships-are intended to enable participants to identify their feelings, take better care of themselves emotionally and make better use of others. We anticipate that the development of these three functions will lead to a lessening dependence on food and make it more possible for participants to change their behaviour. For this reason these three themes are addressed first. The last two themes are improving food choice and increasing activity. They are intended to address obesogenic behaviour by first recognising why participants find lifestyle change so difficult and then enabling them to develop better habits.

Developing emotional intelligence

You may well be familiar with the term 'emotional intelligence' from the book by Daniel Goleman (1995). Here we are particularly concerned with the development of emotional language. There is evidence to suggest that people with eating disorders of all kinds find it difficult to express their feelings in words, a condition known as alexithymia. The relationship between alexithymia 'a default in the ability to identify and express emotions and a prevalence of externally oriented thinking' (Pinaquy et al., 2003) and eating disorders (anorexia and bulimia) has already been demonstrated (Cochrane et al., 1993; Schmidt et al., 1993; de Zwaan et al., 1995; Råstam et al., 1997) however its relationship with obesity has been less researched. Clerici et al. (1992) found a high prevalence of alexithymia in obese people. De Chouly De Lenclave et al. (2001) found that alexithymia was significantly more frequent in obese patients than in controls but that no significant difference was found between patients with and without BED. However Pinaquy et al. (2003) also explored the extent of alexithymia in obese people. They discovered that BED was significantly associated with alexithymia. Since BED affects 20–30% of treatment-seeking obese people (Devlin et al., 1992), this is an important finding. An inability to express emotions is strongly associated with emotional eating which, in turn, Pinaquy et al. found to be a significant predictor of BED.

Our clinical experience has been that some participants in our groups have a great difficulty in finding an emotional language and in articulating their feelings. Without this language it is, of course, difficult to discuss or resolve emotional issues. A person of this kind is thrown back on the use of symbolic behaviour (for example, the use of food) to express what has not been symbolised in words. For these reasons the first step in the process of developing emotional intelligence is the development of an emotional language. Participants will differ in their need for this development.

The programme develops emotional intelligence through a number of exercises designed to expand the emotional lexicon of group members and to get them to be able to identify the syndromes of physical sensations which are named as individual feelings. We have found that, to begin with, the feelings that our participants can identify are those most basic physical sensations such as tired, hungry and thirsty. Over time, and with support, they can identify feelings expressed by others and describe the behaviour which identifies those feelings; so, for example, they can connect anger with shouting and slammed doors and physical violence. They can then begin to identify at least a small range of feelings of their own, especially feelings such as anxiety, guilt and boredom.

We continue the development of emotional intelligence by a number of strategies: one is to ask group members to identify the feelings which trigger overeating. To begin with they often find this difficult. The monitoring sheets which ask them to undertake this exercise are given out in the first few weeks of the programme when many struggle to complete them. However, the exercise has the value of demonstrating just how difficult group members find it to identify and name feelings. It is a good idea to return to the monitoring sheets later in the programme when participants will be better able to use them.

Secondly, we make a point of inviting the expression of feelings about the group experience at the beginning of every session. It is part of the group leader's task to ensure that she creates an environment of safety within which group members can feel free to experiment with voicing their feelings. The group leader needs to be particularly alert to facilitating the expression of negative feelings since they tend to be the feelings which prompt overeating (see pp. xix–xx). It is particularly important that the group leader helps participants to tolerate their wish for rapid results and their disappointment in the inevitably slow process of change. Enduring negative or difficult feelings without having recourse to food is an essential skill in changing eating behaviour and lifestyle.

Thirdly, we invite participants to reflect upon their experience, particularly their experience of mothering, nurture and relationship generally. The experiential exercises which are the vehicle for this task often produce a great deal of emotion. Provided that the emotion can be appropriately contained (see pp. 19–22), we consider that the expression of emotional upset for obese women is valuable in itself since it is our experience that they frequently short circuit emotion and respond to their experience via their eating behaviour. Once emotion has become overt and expressed within the group it can then be shared, discussed and processed. In this way group members are progressively educated in the possibility that feelings can be tolerated, managed and even resolved with the help of other people, through talking, and without the use of food. As the group progresses, it becomes commoner for participants to share with the group examples of the expression of strong emotion rather than examples of bingeing. All of this, of course, is only possible while the group leader models empathic understanding and acceptance.

We extend the strategy of encouraging group members to reflect upon their experience into the fields of food choice and activity. Our experience has been that group members are well aware of what they 'should' eat and that they 'should' be more active. Rather than exhortation to put this latent knowledge into action, we have taken time to enquire about the emotional history of their food choices and their sedentary way of life. Very often we have found that enabling the expression of feeling in relation to these areas has enabled participants to take much greater responsibility for their behaviour in the present. They begin to distinguish better between then and now.

Developing the capacity to self-nurture

It is by no means a new idea that disordered eating has a relationship to difficulties in taking care of oneself. For many participants the only mode of nurturing they knew was to feed themselves. The feeding of the baby is the prototypical example of the connection between love and food (Gerhardt, 2004). This association continues for very many people throughout their lives. Certainly our participants could articulate very clearly how food and love were often connected in their experience even when other modes of the expression of love were absent (Buckroyd et al., in preparation c).

However, many participants had an additional reason to identify nurture with food; for them experience had shown that those on whom they might be supposed to be able to depend, could not be relied upon for consistent nurture. Their solution had been to use food instead. One of our tasks, in relation to these participants, was to validate their ingenuity and capacity for survival while simultaneously suggesting that nurture might also take other forms.

As we have already discussed, our understanding is that our participants are using food to manage their emotional lives and we have also suggested that they have no other way. We are asking them to take part in a group which explores their feelings, but are simultaneously asking them to give up their habitual way of managing feelings. Our long-term aim is to help them to learn to use other people but first they need to learn how to use themselves. We want to prevent participants being overwhelmed by their feelings and memories because we share the view of current trauma experts in thinking that such experiences can simply retraumatise rather than enable the integration of the experience.

This is not the place to discuss the subject of the integration of trauma but we believe it is very important for group leaders to be well informed about it. Herman (1992), Matsakis (1994) and Mollon (1996) are good guides to the subject. Nor are we suggesting that the programme is capable of doing enough psychological work in a group setting to heal serious trauma. We want to propose rather that group members can be helped to control the degree of affect to which they expose themselves using affect management. Group leaders should ensure that they are well informed on this subject (e.g. Zlotnick et al., 1997; Omaha, 2004, www.april-steele.ca/nurturing.php, www.april-steele.ca/self.php, www.sensorymotorpsychotherapy.org/articles.html).

Omaha's Affect Management Skills Training, for example, is a strategy to try to put in place some of the most basic capacities for self-soothing and regulation of affect: 'a formulaic approach to remediating impaired affect regulation resulting from childhood deficit experience' (2004). These skills are taught early in the programme for use, not just during the programme but at any time.

We also consider that it is helpful for participants to be taught the basic outline of how affect management is internalised in ordinary situations and how it is distorted in difficult situations. We have decided to give an outline of these processes for group leaders since the literature describing them is complex. What follows gives a brief account of how a child in a good situation learns affect management.

- In the beginning the child is entirely contained psychologically within the mother (see Figure 3.1). The child's difficult feelings (hunger, pain, anger) are entirely managed by the mother. So, for example, a hungry child who cries is picked up by the mother, soothed and fed.

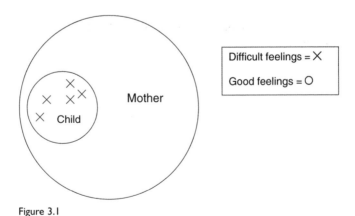

Figure 3.1

- At a slightly later stage of development, the mother soothes the distressed child and down-regulates the feelings but is herself capable of managing her own feelings (see Figure 3.2).

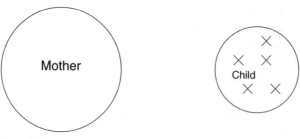

Figure 3.2

- Over time the mother takes in the child's upset feelings and returns them to the child as soothed feelings (see Figure 3.3).

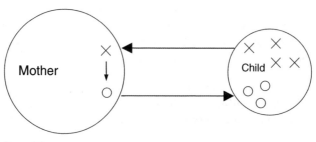

Figure 3.3

- Over time this system becomes internalised within the child and leads to unconscious automatic emotional regulation (see Figure 3.4).

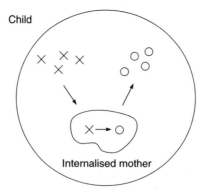

Figure 3.4

A person who has gone through this process in her early life is capable of affect management in all ordinary circumstances.

On the other hand, when early circumstances are not good, the mother is incapable of facilitating the process of affect regulation.

- At The child is not contained within the mother but is felt to be separate, and both mother and child are full of difficult feelings (see Figure 3.5).

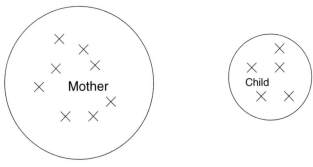

Figure 3.5

- The effect on the mother, who is incapable of managing the child's feelings, is that she feels that the child gives her its feelings and that she will return them unmodified. So, for example, an angry child may have its own angry feelings returned to it, with interest, by an angry mother (see Figure 3.6).

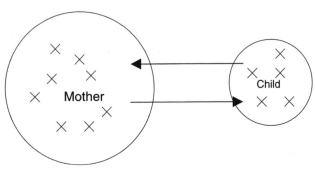

Figure 3.6

- The effect of this process on the child is an emotional numbing or switching off from the parts of the self holding the memories of emotional overwhelm and an internalised mother, full of difficult feelings. The result is a person who is at risk of encountering memories of overwhelm without an internalised system of emotional regulation (Figure 3.7).

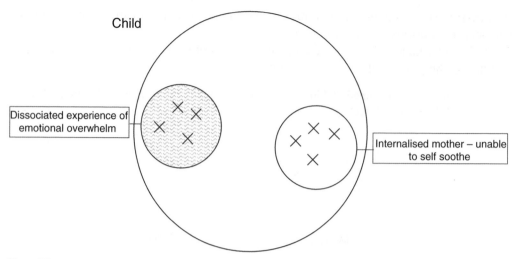

Child

Dissociated experience of emotional overwhelm

Internalised mother – unable to self soothe

Figure 3.7

These skills, collectively, are ways of enabling group members to manage feelings and to resist being overwhelmed by memories so that they are no longer in the present. As a strategy it relies on the idea of an adult self which can take care of hurt child parts.

When participants have affect management skills at their disposal, the process of developing the capacity for self-nurture depends, first of all, on supporting participants in the exploration of how they perceived the nurturing they had received, so that a considerable amount of time is spent using experiential exercises to help them to identify their experience of their mothers, other family members, friends and their support network in general. We begin by asking group members to reflect upon their experience of family mealtimes. Our reasoning is that these occasions provide a snapshot of the family dynamic and an opportunity to identify the quality of the relationships within the family. This exercise (which is often very powerful) also connects food and nurture and frequently demonstrates how charged the subject of food and eating has been for the participants for many years.

We follow the family mealtime exercise with work on mothers. The principal exercise asks participants to create an image of themselves and their mother/principal caregiver, using art materials. The choice of a non-verbal medium is deliberate. As art therapists have always known, the creation of an image can express ideas that are not yet in consciousness. It is a particularly useful strategy for those who would otherwise use food (Buckroyd, 1994; Dokter, 1994; Hinz 2006). Reflection by the group members on the images they have produced offers a strategy for voicing thoughts and feelings about their nurture of which many will previously have been unaware.

These exercises are the preliminary to inviting the group to consider how they nurture themselves and other people. We have found that our participants very often give others a quality of care which they neither received, nor give themselves. The next step therefore is to encourage them in better physical and emotional self-care. We ask them to identify in detail qualities of a good mother or a good friend and to consider when and from whom they had received that sort of care. Too often we have heard stories from women who have little experience of being loved, cherished and valued in the past or the present. However, we have also been able to get group members to identify those in their lives in the past who have supported them (e.g. teachers, best friend's mother, etc.) and those in the present on whom they can rely for support.

Our next task in the development of the capacity to self-nurture is to resurrect their hope that other people may offer them what they long for. We will discuss the process of developing trust in others and hope in relationships in the next section.

However, until our participants have a better sense of their own value, they are incapable of using other people. A further aspect of self nurture is therefore the development of improved self-esteem and body esteem which have been seen as useful components of a psychological approach to obesity (Garner & Wooley, 1991). Lewis et al. (1992) found that group therapy directed at improving self-assertion, self-efficacy and self-esteem enabled group members to improve their scores in these areas but also enabled sustained weight loss. Although the group members were not obese, these results are never the less suggestive. Foreyt and Goodrick (1994) agree that improving self-esteem should be a large part of the treatment of obese people. Morrison (1999) confirmed what is clinically well known, that trying to decrease the value placed upon body shape and size as a means of improving women's self-esteem, is extremely difficult but Wardle et al. (2001) demonstrated that a reduction in body dissatisfaction was associated with a reduction in binge eating score for obese women.

Awareness of the value of improved self-esteem and psychological welfare in general has led a substantial number of researchers to explore the value of an intervention for overweight people which focuses on improving psychological welfare rather than on weight loss. This approach has been strengthened by the discovery of the many physiological and psychological mechanisms which make deliberate weight loss via restriction of intake so difficult. Unfortunately non-dieting approaches do not, generally, lead to significant weight loss and may even reject the concept of weight loss as irrelevant (e.g. Roughan et al., 1990; Garner & Wooley, 1991; Polivy & Herman, 1992; Carrier et al., 1994; Omichinski & Harrison, 1995; Ciliska, 1998; Tanco et al., 1998; Cogan & Ernsberger, 1999; McFarlane et al., 1999). We support the idea of improving self-esteem and psychological welfare but we wish to combine this process with strategies known to produce weight loss and improved health. It is for this reason that we include attention to food choice and increased activity in our programme.

Our strategy for improving self-esteem is, first of all, the maintenance by the group leader of a contained environment of careful listening, consistent concern, acceptance of group members' communications and appropriate challenge. It has been surprising and distressing for us to realise how many of our group members have never expressed their deepest concerns and hurts to anyone. An empathic response from the group leader and the group was in itself validating for many of them.

We begin to address the issue of body esteem in the middle of the programme because by then we anticipate that the group has developed enough trust and cohesion for this very difficult issue to be raised. Group members are asked to identify the messages about their body that they received throughout their growing up and as adults. The aim is to demonstrate that these messages have come from outside and have been internalised and that, therefore, they can be challenged as to whether they are true or not. This work is continued by exploring the meanings attached to fat and thin in order to start to erode the rigid definitions of fat as bad and thin as good. We then ask participants to identify the qualities they value in other people and point out that being thin has not appeared on their list. We move from this to asking them to identify their own positive qualities. As part of the process of imagining change, as a preliminary to enacting it, we ask participants to answer the question: "If you really loved your body what difference would it make to your behaviour?" We urge our group members to deconstruct the cultural messages about fat and thin from TV, magazines, etc., and to create a loving image of the 'acceptable me'. We challenge what may well be a deeply ingrained idea that living has to be deferred until they are thinner. We teach our group members to alter the self-talk that makes disparaging comments about their own bodies, and we ask them to construct a list of what they are grateful for in their bodies – a kind of thank you for its functioning.

A further opportunity for addressing body image concerns is created by the introduction of work on activity, two-thirds of the way through the programme. We are concerned to investigate the group members' experience of activity throughout their growing up. The humiliation suffered by many of our group members who were already fat when called upon to participate in physical activity at school has often contributed to their lack of body esteem. We encourage participants to re-evaluate their capacity for movement while acknowledging the hurts from the past. We support the development of a new vision of their physicality. Both weight loss and increased activity will promote improvements in body esteem.

One of the fundamental strategies we have used throughout the programme is that of empowerment. As a generalisation we would say that our group members feel themselves to be disempowered – the victims of their own lives. The theories of Albert Bandura have been useful in conceptualising the value of identifying and validating success. When group members feel that they have accomplished something, and that their achievement is recognised, their sense of self is enhanced. It is part of the task of the group leader to be watching out for examples of achievement however small and to ensure that they are acknowledged.

Developing relationships

The fundamental hypothesis about food use that we have evolved for working with the population of binge and emotional eaters is that food is used for affect regulation. We think that the reason why weight loss programmes eventually lead to renewed weight gain is that the prior function of the eating behaviour was to enable day-to-day emotional management (see pp. xix–xxii). When changes in eating behaviour are imposed (rather than developing organically) then the person must find other means of managing her feelings or, in due course, the use of food for that purpose will be resumed. This pattern is not necessarily obvious and is often unconscious. Weight loss programmes do not, usually, attend to this issue and therefore when the immediate support of the group or programme comes to an end, individuals are left to their own devices and are highly likely to return to the mode of affect regulation most familiar to them, namely food use.

The support from any weight loss programme is useful. Its termination brings support to an end and may explain why weight regain seems to be delayed until the end of that support system following on from a more active intervention (Jeffery et al., 2000; Perri, 1998, 2002). Research of this kind has led some researchers to propose that obesity should be treated as a chronic condition similar, perhaps, to diabetes (Perri, 1998; NHLBI, 1998; Liebbrand & Fichter, 2002). This solution would, of course, have enormous financial implications, and for that reason, if for no other, alternative avenues need to be explored. A major aim of our groups is to use the group leader and the group to demonstrate the value of other people for affect regulation and to teach participants how to apply the use of people to other circumstances. Rabinor (2004) quotes a group member saying "I took the group in my pocket" (p. 257); this is just the result we are trying to effect. Steptoe et al. (1998) drew attention to the value of social support for people under stress who are otherwise likely to use food to manage it, and Hayward et al. (2000) emphasised the value of support networks for weight loss.

The programme, therefore, has, as one of its main aims, the replacement of food with relationship and human interaction. This is bound to be part of the function of any therapy group but the vast majority of such groups are not working exclusively with people whose means of expressing themselves has been via food. We consider that, by definition, a person who uses food extensively for affect regulation is unable to use words or people for that purpose and needs to learn to do so. It is for this reason that our groups are semi-structured rather than unstructured. The activities presented in the group offer an easier route to interaction than an unstructured group (Buckroyd, 1994).

The whole structure of the group, as well as the content, encourages an ongoing experience of, and reflection upon, relationship with others. Many of our group members were in their 30s and 40s and so had many years of experience of substituting food for people. We recognised that in order to modify this pattern of behaviour, we needed to provide as intense an experience of the usefulness of other people as possible. Thirty-six sessions is not a long programme to undo the habit of decades.

The group leader needs to be aware of how each group member is functioning within the group and to encourage all to participate. She should not wait for the group, or individuals within it, to address failure to participate, or to monopolise the group. If she seriously considers the group members' lack of hope or trust in each other, she will recognise that until trust is well developed she will have to take the role of the protector and facilitator. In due course she can expect that the group will begin to develop these functions, but it will probably be slow to do so.

This group, like any other, will have stages of development. The first will be the establishment of the group itself with its rules for functioning and its focus. In this period, group members will recognise that they have much in common with others and will develop sufficient trust to be able to move on to the next stage. This next stage is the time during which the group members can focus on what brought them to the group and do the work that is necessary for them to begin to change. In our groups that means: reflecting on their eating behaviour, thinking about how they have used food historically, making concrete plans to modify their behaviour, identifying major psychological issues in their lives and starting to address them. This is followed by the development of a greater trust which moves them on from their earlier dependence on the group leader to a greater willingness to interact with each other and, even, to challenge each other. During this period you might expect to see significant changes in relationships within the family, significant behavioural changes and the development of greater hope and autonomy. The final stage is the ending of the group. Over a period of at least six weeks and perhaps up to twice that time, members will begin to recognise that the group will be ending. This truth will provoke a far more overt expression of feelings of all kinds than would have been possible at the beginning of the group. Members will express a wide range of feelings that are likely to include anger and disappointment as well as gratitude and hope.

The process of developing greater trust and reliance on others needs to be addressed in as many ways as possible during the life of the group. For that reason a wide range of different formats are used to enable interaction between group members in many different combinations. Throughout the programme there are opportunities for the group to engage in an activity together. For example:

- *Brainstorming* – This allows individuals to contribute to a group task while at the same time benefiting from the contribution of other members to the same task.
- *Group discussion* – This is a more sophisticated way of demonstrating that other people can make a contribution to each others' understanding.
- *Individual activity discussed in the group* – Individual group members can carry out a task on their own, e.g. painting, and then both share what they have done with other group members and hear what they have to say.

There are also many opportunities for group members to work together in pairs or in small groups. For example:

- Discussing a homework task already completed, in pairs.
- Sharing their history in relation to a topic raised in the session.
- Devising a response to a problem or task.

All of these activities are intended to structure interactions between people who are not used to intimacy with others and who need practice in expressing themselves verbally. They also need practice in being listened to. It has been our experience that, as time goes on, group members become progressively more able to share their experience, even when that is painful, and much more able to name feelings.

The content of the programme also encourages group members to consider their relationships both in the past and in the present. Relationships in the family of origin are explored in a number of exercises which encourage participants to reflect on the nature of those relationships and their effects in the present. We also encourage participants to reflect on their support networks in the present and to consider how they can be improved and extended.

Our group encourages members to contact each other outside group meetings for the specific purpose of mutual support. There are some precedents for this strategy in the work of Perri et al. (1992) and Pendleton et al. (2002), but it is directly counter to the requirements of most therapeutic groups. Its rationale (rather similar to the use of a sponsor in 12-step groups) is that the substance (food) is readily and immediately available and that in order to be weaned from it, the alternative of human interaction with trusted others needs to be available.

We have been surprised at the variation in response to this element of the programme. Some groups have enthusiastically embraced the idea and have formed a support group which has outlived the formal group itself. Many participants have made energetic use of texting and have used this as a means to keep in touch with each other between group meetings. However, there have been some groups, and some individuals within groups, who have not wanted to participate in 'buddying' activities. Sometimes we have felt that this is the result of an understandable worry about confidentiality. Other group members have expressed a wish to keep the group and its activities entirely separate from their social lives. Still others have been anxious about whether a telephone call might be experienced as intrusive or demanding. One or two participants have voiced exactly that reaction and said that they didn't feel able to cope with any emotional demands from anyone else. We remain undecided about the whole idea of 'buddying'. We think that for some people it is the way to friendship and closeness of a kind they have never previously experienced. For others, perhaps with difficult experience of relationship, the whole idea is too threatening and some are simply just not interested. We suggest that you introduce the idea to your group members at a point when they are starting to feel more confident with each other. We have placed this at Session 5 but you may wish to wait longer.

We must also report, however, that all of the groups which have so far completed the programme have made plans to continue to meet. We do not yet know how many people took part in these continuing informal groups nor how long their meetings will continue, but we believe that the wish to meet is a tribute to the positive experience of other people that the groups have given them. We know from research carried out by Latner (2001) that self-help groups are a 'promising venue for the provision of continuing care' and 'an adjunct to more intensive, specialty therapies'.

Improving food choice

The middle section of the programme – that is, Sections 13–24 – has improving food choice as its continuing theme. There is abundant evidence, accumulated over at least the past 20 years, that dietary restriction does not produce sustained weight loss for most people (see pp. xv–xvi). Eating less than we want or need seems to be impossible to sustain by willpower alone for more than a very limited period. The alternative, again understood for at least the past 20 years, is an improvement in food choice (Garner & Wooley, 1991). There is freely available information on what, in the eyes of current nutritional expertise, is seen as a good diet. It can be briefly outlined as a diet high in complex carbohydrate and low in fat and sugar. We have no doubt that our participants understand the basic principles very well and often have an extensive knowledge of food values. For this reason our programme does not include any substantial teaching or information about the constituents of a good diet. Rather, our aim is to make conscious what may be latent knowledge of appropriate eating patterns and to challenge participants on the difference between their knowledge of what they should eat and their actual eating behaviour. We also work on identifying the emotional meaning of particular foods in an attempt to reduce attachment to what may be unsuitable choices.

We begin with an exercise which asks group members to write down what they believe to be a healthy diet for themselves for one day and, when they have done this, to explain why they think it is a good diet. We follow this by asking them to write down what they ate the previous day. The often striking contrast between these two diets is used to raise the issue of why they don't do what they know is good for them. We follow this with an invitation to identify opportunities for modifying inappropriate eating. This cognitive and behavioural approach is followed by an exploration of the food they ate in their family of origin and their current view of it. We ask them how far what they eat now replicates the food in their family of origin and whether that is a conscious choice. Our challenge to them to improve their food choices is accompanied by an exercise on problem solving. All of this material conforms to a standard behavioural and cognitive way of addressing food choice.

We then try to go a little further in identifying meanings and associations to food, both good and bad. These relics from the past may well be still active in influencing food choices. We urge participants to take responsibility for their choices in the present and to think of improving their diet as taking power over food and looking after themselves better. These themes are continued in the discussion of shopping and its problems.

This direct discussion of food choices is supplemented throughout the programme by meal planning strategies. We have discovered that meal planning can be helpful to women who feel afraid of being hungry and who are less compulsive about food if they can provide it for themselves at frequent structured intervals.

Increasing activity

The last 12 weeks of the programme have increased activity as a continuing theme. In what follows here, we describe some of the literature which demonstrates the value of exercise for obese people. We then go on to explain how we included attention to our participants' memories and associations to exercise as a necessary preliminary to changing behaviour. We then briefly review the different options for increasing activity among obese people before describing our use of stepometers.

Research seems to have demonstrated that when exercise is combined with reduced calorific input then the results in terms of weight loss are better than if either strategy had been adopted alone (Miller et al., 1997; Wing & Jakicic, 2000). However, we are concerned not only with weight loss but with maintained weight loss. Again, research shows that those who eat moderately, remain vigilant about their weight, and continue to exercise, are likely to maintain weight loss (Pronk & Wing, 1994; Klem et al., 1997; Wing & Klem, 2002). However, to introduce exercise into the lives of obese women and expect that this change will be maintained is to hope for a lifestyle change that will take months to consolidate.

It seems that many obese women are almost completely inactive; it is likely that they are co-terminus with the 20–30% of least active and most unfit members of the adult population. This group has at least a doubled risk of mortality (Blair & Connelly, 1996). It is now well established that 'sedentary living leads to coronary heart disease and perhaps to some cancers, stroke, non-insulin-dependent diabetes mellitus and other health problems' (Blair & Connelly, 1996). Data from the United States suggests that both adolescent and adult females exercise less than males. For both adolescent and adult women, obesity is one of the most important public health challenges (Maiese, 2002), but although in theory it is possible to be fit and fat (Brodney et al., 2000) these levels of exercise are unlikely to be achieved by obese people (Shaw et al., 2002).

Very few of our group members were active and some were so disabled by their obesity (and sometimes other disabilities) that they were unable to walk, let alone engage in activity. They found even the idea of activity embarrassing and uncomfortable. They were unwilling to go to the gym (hardly surprising since most gyms seem to cater for the young and slender). The thought of going to a swimming pool and putting on a bathing costume was anathema to them.

Popular television shows seem to have taken on none of these considerations and their participants are frequently shown being coerced into activity that is plainly beyond their capacity and distressing to them. For example, one participant in such a show remarked after a gruelling and unsuitable exercise period that she could not imagine people enjoying exercise. We are puzzled by programmes requiring exercise that is plainly unsuitable. It is hard to avoid the conclusion that the exercise is designed as a humiliating spectacle for the TV audience rather than as a genuine attempt to encourage increased activity in overweight people, since it is known that participation in physical activity is influenced by, among other things, levels of discomfort and enjoyment (King et al., 1988). There is little information available on exercise for significantly overweight people. Publishers of exercise manuals have so far not recognised the need for specialised approaches to this group.

Having said all of this, the benefits of exercise for inactive, overweight people are so substantial that it seems well worth while considering how it can be made part of our group members' lifestyle.

Physical benefits

Physical benefits of even moderate levels of activity are substantial. Risk of mortality declines as rates of activity increase and even low to moderate exercise intensity improves coronary artery disease risk factors. These benefits are particularly valuable for those who are sedentary (Blair & Connelly, 1996). Pescatello and VanHeest (2000) demonstrated that "lifestyle physical activity" benefited cardio-metabolic health among obese people even when weight loss was not substantial. A total of 30 minutes moderate activity undertaken on three or more days per week was suggested to be enough to reduce the risk of cardiovascular disease substantially (ACSM, 1995). However, more recent consensus (Saris et al., 2003; Schoeller et al., 1997) suggests that "prevention of weight regain in formally obese individuals requires 60–90 minutes of moderate intensity activity [per day] or lesser amounts of vigorous intensity activity" (Saris et al., 2003, p. 101). Whether this is an attainable goal is another question, however, any activity will have desirable effects. Mobility is improved, with a corresponding decrease in aches and pains and metabolic rate is increased with a corresponding benefit for calorific consumption. Appetite is reduced through lowering of insulin levels.

In order to **lose** weight, as opposed to maintaining weight loss, group members would need to undertake vastly more exercise than these relatively minimum amounts. A review by Miller et al. (1997) concluded that exercise programmes were not effective in producing weight loss compared to diet alone or exercise and diet, but even a small increase in activity will help to maintain weight loss, or go some way to stabilising existing weight (Shaw et al., 2002). In terms of obesity even stabilising of weight can be seen as a positive outcome.

Psychological benefits

The psychological benefits of increased activity are also substantial. The release of endorphins promotes improved mood and reduces depression. The successful undertaking of activity promotes empowerment and self-efficacy and, thus, improvements in self-esteem (Shaw et al., 2002).

Changing attitudes and behaviour

All of this is well known and well understood. The problem is how a group of seriously overweight and almost completely inactive women can be supported to improve their activity levels when it is known that overweight people have particular difficulty maintaining exercise (Wing & Jakicic, 2000). What change needs to take place to allow them to begin to move more? Our first answer to this question is that women have to get over the feelings and associations to exercise that they carry with them. It is known that, by puberty, most girls have ceased to engage in physical activity (Goran et al., 1998). Sport is seen as unfeminine and the usual accompaniments of unflattering sports wear and activity taking place in public, when girls are acutely self-conscious and conscious of their bodies, are not likely to recommend it. Many of our participants had excruciating memories of humiliation and embarrassment from school sport. We felt it was necessary to get all these feelings out of the way before we could start to talk about increasing activity in the present.

It was then necessary to evaluate the group members' readiness for change using the Prochaska and DiClemente model of change. Identifying their place in the change process meant that individuals could be encouraged to move along that process rather than assume that they were ready to increase their activity (Wing & Jakicic, 2000).

We now need to mention the issues of vocabulary. 'Sport' and 'exercise' are often taken to refer to organised and formalised activity. For most of our participants this kind of activity was out of the question. Indeed, in common with current usage, we talked not about exercise but about activity. The question was what sort of activity might they undertake?

We ended up with two solutions to that problem, both of them 'home based activities' or 'lifestyle exercises' (Wing & Jakicic, 2000). Rather than participate in supervised exercise, an attempt was made to get our participants to increase activity without doing so in a formal way and without going anywhere or using any special equipment. Activity accumulated over the day is effective in delivering health benefits (Wing & Jakicic, 2000). We tried to encourage our group members to come up with their own ideas about how that could be done in the spirit of empowering them and encouraging them to take ownership of the changes, but the kinds of thing that we imagined were: going up and down stairs more often; not using the television remote control; getting things for themselves rather than asking others to get them, and so on. Perri et al. (1997) demonstrated that, at 15 months home-based exercise showed superior performance, better adherence and significant weight losses than group exercise.

Our other solution was to provide participants with stepometers. We were influenced by research which indicates that walking is probably the best and simplest all-round cardiovascular exercise for all of us, and is particularly valuable for those suffering from Type 2 diabetes (Yamanouchi et al., 1995; Morris & Hardman, 1997; Manson et al., 2002). It has the added advantage that it costs nothing and is universally available. These were important considerations to the group members who had very little in the way of financial resources. It does create a problem for women who are unable to walk. We encouraged those group members to find themselves a programme of exercise which would at least maintain some joint mobility even though it was not load bearing. One group developed sufficient cohesion to be able to take a non-mobile member of the group swimming with them and were brave enough to get the hoist used to enable the disabled member to get in and out of the pool. However, these are complex and time-consuming operations and not to be expected.

As a way of creating targets for increasing activity we gave all our members stepometers. Lean (2005), in the USA, noted that walking an extra 2,000 steps a day combined with a small decrease in consumption could abolish 90% of obesity. We followed the advice of Cooper et al. (2003) as to which stepometer to buy and found that the Yamax SW200 was very accurate and worked well. We thought about merely lending it to our members but it cost only about £10 when bought in bulk and we felt it was a means to encouraging members to continue with their walking after the intervention was complete. With the stepometers we could create a base line of each individual's activity and use that as the starting point for an increase. We were pleased with the excitement and pleasure that the stepometers gave and the generally enthusiastic reception for them as a device to help increase activity. At the time of writing it seems as if most participants have maintained a higher level of activity.

Chapter 4
Description of the Research Programme

Introduction

As you, the reader, will have recognised by this point, we write this book from the perspective of two therapists who have worked extensively with eating disordered and obese women. Our original training was in psychodynamic thinking and although we have since modified our approach so that we draw our treatment strategies from a wide range of theories, we find it easy to identify emotional meaning in eating behaviour.

Food can never be simply the means to satisfy hunger in human societies. Its absolute necessity for our survival gives it an importance way beyond the casual acceptance of plenty that we experience. Our experiences with food as babies and children are laden with meaning and association that influence us as adults. Although environmental factors which render food cheap and readily available undoubtedly have a part to play in the current levels of obesity, we are also struck by how its availability allows it to be used as a symbol and a remedy. We see no difference conceptually speaking between psychologically generated obesity and other disordered eating such as anorexia or bulimia. Overeating or under eating, bingeing or starving, seem to us to have more in common than they are different. There is a general consensus that anorexia and bulimia are multiply determined but that one element in them is emotional. We understand the overeating that leads to obesity in exactly the same way.

Since 1999 we have been engaged in developing a research programme to test some of our ideas. In particular we are investigating whether attending to the emotional meanings of food for individual women who binge eat, eat emotionally and have difficult histories and poor attachment patterns, enables them to modify their eating behaviour and achieve sustained weight loss. We are well aware that the clinical experience of those working solely from this perspective has demonstrated that women improve on measures such as self-esteem and depression but they do not lose weight. However, our hypothesis is that if known effective methods of weight loss (diet, exercise and CBT) are combined with a psychotherapeutic element then the psychological purposes which have maintained overeating may be sufficiently eroded and other strategies for affect management may be sufficiently implemented, to permit maintained weight loss.

Our research programme began with preliminary studies to develop an intervention. We are currently engaged in the first of three Phase 2 studies to explore the gross effect of the intervention with three different populations. We hope, in due course, to be able to run a Randomised Controlled Trial. At the same time we are carrying out a number of auxiliary studies which explore further the relationship between emotional issues and eating behaviour. Although our work has, to date, been carried out with obese women we believe that there is an emotional component in all eating behaviour and that bingeing and emotional eating are part of many women's behaviour (we are less sure about men). We think that a psychological component would be useful in all weight management programmes, even those that are preventive or that deal with people who are overweight rather than obese. We suspect, as the research we have cited suggests, that this might be a useful perspective in working with obese children and young people and their families. We hope that in due course we will be able to test some of these ideas.

Preliminary studies

The preliminary studies that we carried out have been described at some length elsewhere (Buckroyd et al., 2006). Here we will give a brief outline. The first study explored whether a psychotherapeutic element added to a cognitive behavioural programme to modify binge eating, produced psychological and behavioural changes likely to lead to sustained weight loss. The results showed changes in attitudes to eating which, if maintained, were likely to lead to sustained weight loss. Kern et al. (2002) used a similar strategy for estimating treatment success. Numbers in our study were very small but the results were sufficiently encouraging for us to test the intervention (psychotherapy + CBT) with a further group of obese women. Six of the eight completers showed maintained weight loss at 18 month follow-up.

This research had a number of weaknesses but was sufficiently encouraging for us to continue our work. After reviewing the literature, we were persuaded by the research evidence of the value of diet, exercise and behavioural approaches for weight loss. We therefore included those elements in our next intervention, which is described in this book.

Current research

Since 2005 we have been testing this new intervention with groups of obese women. This is the work that is described in the accompanying programme. There is more detail of exactly how the groups were run in Chapter 6, and, of course, the content is described in great detail in Part II.

Group therapy for women who binge eat

This study was one of the group of studies which we have carried out to explore further the relationship between emotional issues and eating behaviour. It offered a six-month group for obese women who were binge eaters (Seamoore et al., 2006). Eight women attended a weekly integrative therapy group. At six-month follow up all participants demonstrated changes in eating behaviour of statistical significance. Reduction in binge eating was accompanied by changes in dichotomous thinking, greater awareness of eating behaviour, greater detachment from food and dietary changes. Although this study placed less emphasis on improving food choices and increasing activity than the programme described in this book, the CBT and psychotherapeutic elements had many similarities. Weight changes were not reported for this group but it is reasonable to assume that changes in attitude reported will lead to sustained weight loss. Issues such as the necessary length of a group of this kind and whether it needs to include material on food choice and increased activity have not, as yet, been researched. Our feeling is that weight gain developed over a good number of years is unlikely to be reversed and maintained in a short time, however desirable that would be for funders.

Obese people's understanding of their eating behaviour

There is a lack of studies which investigate obese people's own understanding of their eating behaviour and attempts at weight loss. We undertook a study of this kind (Bidgood & Buckroyd, 2005) which confirmed the experience of prejudice and stigmatisation reported by other researchers. It also revealed that excessive eating can feel like addiction; that prejudice and stigmatisation restrict lifestyles and hinder treatment; that dieting has limited success; that our participants felt unheard; and that they needed ongoing help. Their self-esteem was uniformly poor. This study confirms the findings of other qualitative investigations (e.g. Lyons, 1998; Goodspeed-Grant & Boersma, 2005) and has strengthened our resolve to develop interventions that respond to the needs of service users.

Population study

It is already known that emotional eating and binge eating correlate (Eldredge & Agras, 1996; Telch & Agras, 1996) and that binge eating is characteristic of up to 46% of obese people (Marcus & Wing, 1987; Gluck et al., 2004). Furthermore it is known that binge eating is associated with weight regain (Fichter et al., 1993; Foreyt & Goodrick, 1994; Agras et al., 1997). What is not known is how emotional eating and binge eating relate to BMI within the general population. It seems likely that there is a continuum from little or no binge and emotional eating for people of normal weight to greatly increased binge and emotional eating for obese people. If this relationship is demonstrated it will provide further evidence that emotional factors need to be considered in the treatment of obese people. We are in the process of researching this hypothesis.

Trauma and attachment difficulties in obese women

Fairburn et al. (1998) demonstrated that women with BED had rates of trauma equal to those in a psychiatric population. We are carrying out a study which compares trauma and attachment difficulties in two groups of women, 60 with a BMI ≥ 35, and 60 women consistently slender for five years. Our hypothesis is that the obese women will show greater levels of trauma and attachment difficulties. Our focus, again, is on the use of such a result for informing treatment options.

Champion slimmers

In association with the BBC we carried out a survey of 74 winners of slimming competitions who were examined with respect to their relationship with food. They had lost an average of 40% of their body weight during dieting. Weight regain after the dieting phase increased as time went on. However, even those who had lost the weight more than five years previously were on average about a third lighter than at the start of their diet.

These relatively good results were modified by measures of disordered eating. The women showed significantly higher levels of emotional eating, eating concern, shape concern, weight concern and restraint than the general population: 70% had binged in the last three months and 31% binged four or more times in the past month. These figures are comparable to the prevalence of bingeing found in those seeking clinical treatment for obesity, despite the fact that only 20% were obese (at the time of data collection). Bingeing was more common among those with high restraint, eating, shape and weight concern. These findings suggest that weight loss by itself is no indication that difficulties with food, shape and size have been overcome. They confirm our conviction that weight loss strategies, for a significant proportion of women, need to be accompanied by attention to psychological issues (Buckroyd et al., in preparation b).

Future intentions

We are currently planning to continue to develop the intervention used in this book for specific populations and hope to win funding to work with morbidly obese diabetic women who fulfil our criteria and also with a student population. We hope that the work we have described above will make a contribution to the search for more successful interventions for obesity. At the moment an obese person has very little chance of sustained weight loss without undergoing surgery. We would like to help develop other alternatives.

Chapter 5

Experience of Running the Treatment Groups

Introduction

In this section we would like to share with you the experience we have gained as a result of running the group programme this book describes. If you are already very experienced in running groups, much of what we say will be familiar to you. However, even though all who were involved in this project had extensive experience, we learned a great deal from carrying out the programme. We hope that what we learned will be useful to you.

Recruitment of group members

An obvious necessary preliminary to running a group of this kind is the recruitment of its members. We would like to share our experience of this process since it may be helpful to others (Buckroyd & Rother, in preparation a). Our initial intention was to run groups for obese women in primary care and to invite health professionals to refer their patients to us. When we made presentations in health centres for this purpose we were given an enthusiastic reception. Health professionals of all kinds assured us that they could immediately think of numbers of patients who would benefit from our proposed treatment, but for reasons that we have never understood, very few referrals were forthcoming. This may be because of the pressure of work, but it puzzles us that a resource which was offered free and enabled conformity with government guidelines on addressing obesity, was virtually ignored. What is more, when patients were referred, as happened with a few energetic health professionals, it seems as though the letter that was sent to patients telling them about the groups and suggesting that they contact us, was often seen as coercive rather than an opportunity. For example, of 17 women referred by a health visitor, only 10 wished to be interviewed. Of these, eight attended the interview, and of these in turn, only six attended the first meeting of the group. Within a few weeks only two women were continuing to attend and, when this group was inevitably amalgamated with another, only one woman made the transition.

Of the 55 women who were interviewed following referral, 33 (60%) joined the group and there were 27 completers (49%). By contrast when we advertised for participants in the local free newspaper, we were overwhelmed with responses and of the 24 women subsequently interviewed, all 24 attended the first meetings of their group. After the first 12 weeks of the group 20 women were still attending and 18 completed (75%). It seems that the effort required to self-refer implied a greater readiness to use the group process. The moral of the story seems clear: advertising works better in recruiting group members. Unfortunately this recruitment process did not access as many of the population of women in deprived circumstances that we had originally tried to recruit.

The literature on referral is not particularly helpful. Alexander (1998) found that self-referral for an employee assistance programme led to greater satisfaction than referral by a supervisor. On the other hand, Loneck et al. (1996) found that compulsory referral to drug treatments resulted in an outcome as successful as that of clients who entered treatment voluntarily.

Initial contact

Because we were running groups as part of a research programme, the initial contact for potential participants was with the researcher. The process of carrying out measurements, administering questionnaires and conducting an intervie gave an opportunity for inter-viewees to ask questions about the group and implicitly to test out further what they had already learned from the participant information. If the group is not being conducted as a research project, other strategies will have to be developed for an initial meeting. We think that it is very important that potential participants have the chance to discuss the nature of the group and its aims and objectives. We found that even though participants said that they had read the information pack they often did not understand the nature of the programme. In particular we were often asked whether participants would be given a diet sheet – a question which revealed a complete misunderstanding of the programme. We found that participants used this initial meeting as an assessment process; those to whom it was not appealing did not attend the group at all. In future we will also use this initial meeting as an assessment from our point of view, since we now understand so much more clearly how to describe the people for whom our programme is likely to be successful. Benson (2001) suggests making individual contracts with potential members as a way of enabling discussion of motivation, objectives, expectations, responsibility, confidentiality and safety.

Size of group

Traditionally, small therapy groups have a membership of between 7 and 10 (Aveline & Dryden, 1988). Our initial intention was to have groups of up to 12. This decision was based on our feeling that whatever the emotional needs of the membership it was unlikely that they could be sufficiently met in a group meeting for 36 sessions. Our intention was never to attempt the fundamental restructuring that is part of the analytic group therapy purpose (Hyde, 1988) but rather to enable and consolidate lifestyle change. For this reason we fixed on 12 as a manageable number for one group leader who would be able to get to know the participants and create relationships with and within the group that would be significant and enduring. In group theory a group of this size is known as an activity group or a learning group (Benson, 2001). Groups recruited from referred participants suffered badly from drop-out so that we found ourselves running groups for as few as four members. Other clinicians report drop-out from groups is higher than from individual treatment (Gilbert, 2000).

In groups where women self-referred there has been a much lower drop-out rate and both groups settled at 10, so we have had experience of a membership from 4 to 10. Our conclusions are that 12 is slightly too big a group and that 10 would be better. On the other hand, four is too small to provide the energy needed to carry through the programme. A group as small as that makes great demands on the group leader and tends to get very involved in the pathology of individuals in the manner of analytic groups. The concept of the group as facilitating and requiring members to take responsibility for their own lives (Ratigan & Aveline, 1988) is much closer to the ethos of what we were attempting.

McKisack and Waller (1997) report evidence to suggest that additional treatment, e.g. individual as well as group treatment, reduces drop-out in groups for bulimics. A significant number of our participants proved to have difficult personal histories which not only could not be properly addressed in the group but also tended to overwhelm these individuals and have a powerful effect on other group members. As described elsewhere (p. 18–22), we recommend the use of strategies to limit emotional overwhelm, but we think that ongoing individual therapy would be a very valuable resource for some participants. Whether such a comprehensive treatment could be afforded is another matter.

Inclusion and exclusion criteria

Inclusion and exclusion criteria, we now think, should be as follows:

Inclusion

- Female
- Obese BMI ≥ 35
- Readiness to take action in relation to weight as measured by the Prochaska and DiClemente process of change.
- Willingness to join a group
- Ability to understand and process data.
- Showing evidence of binge and/or emotional eating as measured by Gormally et al. (1982) and Arnow et al. (1995) or other appropriate measures.
- Showing evidence of a poor attachment history and/or a history of trauma as measured by the Adult Attachment Interview (George et al., 1996) and the Trauma Interview Schedule (Turner & Lee, 1998) or other appropriate measures.

The groups we ran were limited to females. The issue of obesity treatment for men will be discussed later.

The minimum BMI that we accepted was 30. However, we now think that the minimum should be 35. So many people are overweight that it seems sensible to restrict the provision of an intensive treatment, such as we propose, to the heavier end of the spectrum of obesity. We are currently planning an intervention where the minimum BMI will be 40 but it may be that the same criteria for our treatment should be adopted as for surgery (Mitchell & Courcoulas, 2005) of a minimum of 40, or 35 if there are co-morbidities.

Our initial interview was used partly to determine readiness to take action in relation to weight. However, we did not use any formal means of ascertaining this. We now think that it would be sensible to use Prochaska and DiClemente (see pp. 9-10) to identify the patient's attitude to change more precisely. As we have discovered, attending the initial interview is not in itself a reliable guide to motivation.

Many people have anxieties about being a member of a group. Because a potential participant comes to an interview it does not mean that she has consciously realised that she will be joining a group or that she has considered how she feels about group membership. We think it is important to explore the issue of a group as clearly as possible with each potential participant and, where necessary, to discuss specific anxieties or even suggest that a group may not be appropriate for this individual.

The group demands that participants will be able to read and write English with some fluency. There are clear issues about equal access to treatment in restricting membership to this group. However, at this stage in the development of the treatment we decided to restrict the group and hope that additional work could be done at a later stage to make it accessible to learning disabled people or non-English speakers. There is a particular need for interventions for obese learning disabled people (Turner & Moss, 1996) and for some minority communities such as South Asians who are particularly vulnerable to Type 2 diabetes (Pomerleau et al., 1999). We are not at all sure whether the approach we employ would be transferable to those coming from radically different cultures for whom, for example, individualism and the reflection upon the personal inner world may not be usual. This whole area needs much more research and we have not so far explored it.

Although we used measures to identify bingeing and emotional eating we did not include them as part of the inclusion criteria. We had not at that time conceptualised our ideas about sub-groups of obese people and their treatment as clearly as we have now. We think that measuring these behaviours is essential to identify the patient group for whom this treatment is suitable.

Similarly we did not use attachment and trauma measures but now think that they should be used to identify potential group members.

Exclusion

- Obesity caused by medical conditions or treatment.
- Serious mental health problems.
- Addiction to alcohol or other substances.
- Under 18 years old or over 65.
- Pregnancy.

Because this programme is targeted at people whose obesity is psychogenic it is appropriate to exclude those whose obesity is clearly caused by medical conditions or treatment.

Not everybody has the capacity to tolerate the inevitable limitations of attention available to any one individual in a group. For this reason we decided to exclude those whom we felt were unlikely to be able to manage this situation. Our exclusion of people with serious mental health problems relates to the need to ensure that a group can work effectively together and that the needs of one person do not preoccupy the group. The exclusion of people with addictions, e.g. drugs and alcohol, again relates to the running of the group and the demands of those with co-morbidities. Nevertheless, we have no wish to be discriminatory; it must be the group leader's decision whether she can cope with particular individuals within a group. As we indicated previously, the initial interview is an important opportunity for assessing whether a group is appropriate for any particular individual. As we also mentioned above, it may be appropriate for some people to undertake individual counselling at the same time.

In our current study we included anyone over 18 with no upper age restriction. However, we have since read a correspondence in the *British Medical Journal* (Visvanathan & Chapman, 2005) which has made us question whether it is advisable to include people older than 65 (see also Heiat, 2003). In view of this uncertainty, it may be appropriate to restrict the age range at least until there is more clarity on this subject. We also understand that obesity increases with age, but only until the age of 64 (Rennie & Jebb, 2005). A cut-off at 65 may therefore be supported by the natural history of obesity.

We excluded pregnant women from the group although in practice a number of our participants became pregnant during the course of the group. The exclusion was entirely to do with our research. Our primary measure was weight loss and, clearly, that was impossible to determine when a woman became pregnant. In a non-research setting it might well be quite appropriate to include pregnant women, since the programme is concerned less with achieving immediate weight loss and more with implementing lifestyle changes and changes in attitude to food which are likely to be beneficial to a woman, pregnant or not. However, measuring weight loss would clearly not be appropriate as the primary measure for determining the success of the intervention for these women.

If this intervention were being offered without the complication of a research project, there seems no reason why it should not be combined with other weight loss strategies. It would be interesting to explore, for example, collaborating with a commercial weight loss organisation and leaving them to deal with practical issues of food choice and activity and thus creating more time for the consideration of the CBT and psychotherapy elements of the programme. Commercial weight loss programmes are very good at creating precisely that – weight loss – they are not nearly as good at delivering maintained weight loss. Similarly it might be useful to combine our programme with Orlistat. The drug would enhance weight loss which would probably support motivation while the programme could focus on consolidating lifestyle change. The problem created for the health service by the vast numbers of people who are obese – almost a quarter of the population – means that creative and innovative solutions are all worth exploring.

Will it work for men?

So far we have only had women in our groups and we notice that by far the majority of treatments for obesity are also directed at women. There is something a little odd about this since there are almost as many obese men (22.9%) as obese women (25.4%) (House of Commons Health Committee, 2004). Why then have groups developed for women alone? Part of the answer may be cultural. Until very recently women have been under much more cultural pressure than men to maintain a slender body. Deviation from that preferred norm has been the occasion of enormous shame and distress. As a result women, for most of the past 50 years, have spent increasing amounts of time, resources and energy focused on their body shape (Cogan & Ernsberger, 1999). Even though this seems to be changing, so that men are now being shown idealised body shapes and exhorted to develop that shape (as men's magazines demonstrate), there is still, as far as we can see, much less pressure on men to base their self-esteem on their appearance. Nevertheless, from a health point of view, groups for men would clearly be a good idea.

Our interest in doing this work derives from our experience with working with eating disorders which are certainly very much more common among women than among men. We have extrapolated many of the themes in our programme (e.g. anxieties about body shape and size) from our work with women. Although men may be equally in need of treatment it is not clear to us whether the programme we have developed would be appropriate. It is known that there are cultural inhibitions for men in acknowledging feelings, weakness and vulnerability (Möller-Leimkühler, 2000; Addis & Mahalik, 2003) so it may be that something rather different needs to be developed. Models based on work with alcohol or drug misusers may be more appropriate.

We did consider whether we should recruit mixed groups, but we decided against it because our experience has been, with both eating-disordered and obese women, that they frequently report abusive treatment from men both as children and as adults. We felt that to have a mixed group would be too difficult for the women and perhaps also for the men. As far as we know, these issues to do with male or mixed groups for obese people, have not been researched. When a reliably effective treatment for obese women has been developed, there may be the opportunity to see how it would work in mixed groups or for men alone.

Length of intervention

Whenever we have mentioned the duration of the group in primary care circles we have been met with a sharp intake of breath. Thirty-six sessions each of two hours is thought to be extremely long. However, the group has very ambitious aims which are unlikely to be met by a short intervention. There is a consensus that six months is the minimum time for lifestyle change (Clark & Hampson, 2001). Perri et al. (1988) showed that a 40 week treatment was more effective than a 20 week treatment for both weight loss and maintained weight loss. In addition, as we have discussed, the programme is directed at a group of women who have sustained significant psychological damage, to the extent that they misuse food.

Many obese women have spent 20 years or more getting to their current size and a significant number of them may well have been overweight since childhood. It seems improbable to us that a lifestyle practised for such an extended period will be reversed in a short time. The NHS document, *Commissioning Obesity Services* (NHS Modernisation Agency/NHS Alliance, 2005) declares that 'we need to invest in this area in order to prevent diseases such as diabetes, stroke and heart disease and thereby decrease demand on NHS services. Because obesity disproportionately affects the least well of [sic] there is also a strong argument for targeting services to those with greatest need in order to address inequalities in health.' We believe that services for the patient group we have described, will need to offer long-term interventions.

We fixed the length of our group sessions at two hours. Traditionally group therapy sessions last for an hour and a half (Aveline & Dryden, 1988). However, our groups may be a little larger than the usual eight members of a therapy group. The additional time takes account of the larger numbers, but also of the semi-structured format. The exercises will take up more time than a purely talking group. As you will see from the description of the programme, some sessions use art materials to create an image and others use devices such as structured recall, diagrams and grids and small group work creating lists. These strategies often require extended time.

The very significant drain on NHS resources of conditions associated with obesity (House of Commons Health Committee, 2004) may also justify an intervention which has the potential to reduce that demand. Formal cost/benefit analysis will have to await further completed research data.

Location and layout of group meeting room

We found that the location of the meeting room in the town was a significant issue. Two of the venues were in locations thought by the participants to be unsafe for an evening group. In both cases this was compounded by the need for those who had cars to park some distance away and walk through pedestrian precincts. These are issues that need consideration early in the planning process. Some attention also needs to be given to the location of the group meeting room within the building. The participants may very well have difficulties with mobility. A room that is not accessible will immediately undermine the viability of the group as well as demonstrate the kind of disrespect that we must make every effort to avoid. The room must also be adequately sound-proofed and private.

The layout of the room also needs consideration. Some thought should be given to chairs. Many participants will be unable to fit into chairs with arms and many will find it difficult to get down into, or out of, low chairs. We like to have chairs in a circle but it is useful to have tables available for artwork and other exercises. Small groups may wish to work round a table. It should be remembered that participants are unlikely to be able to draw, among other things, on the floor.

Purpose of the group

One of the better known characteristics of analytic groups is the reluctance of the group leader to explain the purpose of the group – a characteristic that is often felt to be pointlessly frustrating. In our programme the leader, by contrast, has the opportunity to reiterate the aims and objectives of the group which will already have been made known to the members from the written information given to them and the subsequent first contact. Not only does this immediately establish the focus for the group but it also requires members to revisit their motivation for joining the group and to take responsibility for it.

Confidentiality

The expectation in the groups we describe, is that the participants will, in time, disclose a considerable amount about themselves and their experience. Much of this information is of a personal and private nature; for example, group members have talked about their current marital relations, their relations with their children, details of their childhood and upbringing which are often difficult, and material about their eating behaviour which may well be felt to be shameful. Clearly it is necessary that the group constitutes as safe an environment as possible in which to share such material. For this reason the group membership is closed as soon as the group is formed. No late entrants or rolling membership can be permitted. Besides this, the group is following a programme and joining late creates what we think are insuperable problems. To stress the need for safety in the group we have drawn up a formal confidentiality agreement for each of the group members to sign at the first meeting of the group (see Appendix 1).

The group leader has the task of describing what this confidentiality agreement means and needs to stress that if group members get together outside the group meeting, discussion of other members of the group is forbidden. Similarly group members are not allowed to discuss what went on at the group with others, e.g. partners, in any other terms than their own experience of the group. Of course, this agreement is unenforceable but it does give appropriate weight to an important element of the group.

Boundary setting

The importance of commitment to regular attendance and to arriving and leaving on time needs to be stressed. Yalom is eloquent on the effect of absences and lateness (Yalom, 2005). Not only do absent group members miss part of the group process and so find themselves out of step with the group, the group members who are present will find the absence disruptive. Repeated absences are likely to result in either the absent member dropping out, or the group attacking her when she does return. Since an important element in the group process is the development of strong ties between group members, it is desirable that group members should be encouraged to contact anyone who has been absent. We also think that the group leader should contact absentees, after unexplained absences, indicating that they have been missed and that they will be welcomed back at the next group meeting. At the first meeting of the group the group leader should establish how each group member wishes to be contacted. There are some women who emphatically do not wish to be phoned and others for whom that is their preferred method of contact. Similarly the group leader needs to inform members of the group how they can contact her if they are unable to attend. We strongly recommend a direct means of contact, e.g. E-mail or mobile rather than a method of leaving messages. It is our experience that messages do not get passed on and an apparently unexplained absence will have an impact on the group.

As will be apparent, the programme for the group is cumulative, that is to say that later sessions depend on work done in earlier sessions. This structure has implications for absences. Some sessions, e.g. Session 8 on mothers, are critical, in fact the work for this session extends backwards and forwards on either side but missing one or two sessions at this juncture is likely to result in the group member concerned missing an essential step in her own development and in the group process. Group leaders need to be able to advise group members to leave the group if they have missed too much. What 'too much' is, will be a matter for judgement. Our experience has been that there is a difficulty for both the absentee and the rest of the group in reintegrating someone who has not participated sufficiently in the emotional process of the group. It is also the case that group members can find the material in the programme too difficult. As explained earlier, the group leader needs to be very alert to the need to contain the group, to teach affect management and to modify the material as necessary, if drop-out is to be minimised.

Some participants have created situations that mean that they will be repeatedly late to the group. If it appears, after discussion, that the circumstances causing the lateness cannot be changed then, in our opinion, the group member should not be allowed to continue with the group. The disrespect that repeated lateness shows to the group and the disruption of the group process that is involved, erodes the necessary safety and containment of the group. Lateness can also indicate ambivalence about attendance at the group and should therefore be explored. It is also the case that sometimes the bus comes late.

In a group that lasts 36 sessions, it is certain that there will have to be breaks and holidays. The group was originally devised to fit in with school terms so there would be three terms, each of approximately 12 weeks, and each term would be punctuated with a one-week break. One of the purposes of this arrangement was to allow mothers of school age children to attend the group. You may not wish to keep to this academic year format but, whether you do or not, you need to ensure that the dates of breaks are available to group members in written form as early as possible. You may wish to negotiate these with group members at the first meeting or establish dates after the initial interviews have been completed. In either case written confirmation of the dates should be given to all participants as soon as possible. Again, unexpected interruptions or inadequate notice erode safety and trust.

The behaviour of group members needs to be similarly boundaried. It is perhaps unlikely that participants would engage in behaviour that would damage anything in the therapy room or engage in violent or abusive behaviour, but many women have been on the receiving end of violence and abuse. A statement from the group leader stating that such behaviour is not permitted may again enhance the safety of the group. Alternatively, you may wish to create rules with the group. Group members are much more likely to take notice of a code that they have helped to devise. It would be useful to include something about listening respectfully to others and not interrupting. Since these virtues are relatively uncommon, the early sessions of the group include training in listening skills.

An important part of establishing the safety of the group is the conduct of the group leader. We consider the psychoanalytic model of group leadership, which relies a great deal on the initiative of the group and the silence of the group leader (Hyde, 1988), an inappropriate model for the groups we are describing. On the other hand, we also feel that the Rogerian model of a group leader as someone indistinguishable from the group members (Thorne, 1988) is also unsuitable. The group leader has an active role and, although she encourages collaboration and interaction, she is not just another member of the group.

Absences and breaks

In any group the absence of any group member is likely to be disruptive. Breaks for holidays are also difficult to manage, especially earlier in the life of the group. We found that a group which included the long summer break had difficulties resuming work and risked drop-out. We suggest that the group avoids holidays of more than two or three weeks. Bearing in mind the common difficulty of group members in using other people to help manage their experience, the group leader needs to be particularly attentive to the unspoken communication of absence from the group, especially when there is no message from the absent member. We think it is appropriate for there to be a response to the absent member from the group leader, or indeed from the other group members. If the group is being used to model the usefulness of other people, then the group leader must model the expression of interest and concern and must teach the other group members to do the same.

How the group leader communicates with group members, after an absence, needs to be thought through before it happens. The traditional way of communicating in psychotherapeutic circles is via letter. We were working with a group of people to whom communication by letter was very unusual. The only letters they ever received were official communications from agencies such as hospitals or the local authority. Their own favourite mode of communication was via text. We discussed early in the group process how they would like to be contacted. None of them said by letter; they preferred to be telephoned or texted, so that is what we did.

Initial equipment for group members

One of the things we have wanted to do in establishing these groups has been to give members some symbol of our respect for their courage in attending the group. For this purpose we have provided each participant with a notebook, a pen and an envelope file. These can be personalised before they are distributed, if you wish. Some group members have been a little wary of these gifts because they have been afraid that the group would 'be like school', but generally they seem to have valued the gesture. Even if participants have made relatively little use of these materials, we have noticed that they have been faithfully carried backwards and forwards. We noticed a similar phenomenon in the group that we ran in the preliminary studies, where the self-help book was brought to the groups and taken home again. In psychodynamic theory, things that are associated with the therapist can have a useful function of enabling the participant to bear her in mind – the so-called transitional object (Winnicott, 1953). We have also provided name labels for both group members and the group leader. We have asked them to be worn for the first few weeks until names become known. Anything that expresses respect and concern for the comfort and ease for the participants in the early stages of the group, is desirable.

Listening skills

The successful running of the group demands that group members listen to each other. Since this is not a skill that is generally practised, we use the opportunity of the first meeting to conduct a listening skills exercise similar to the sort of thing that might be taught in a counselling skills course. Because the group is semi-structured and focused on content with relevance to obesity, group members are not, primarily, directed towards the experience of being with other people as they would be in a conventional therapy group (Yalom, 2005). Rather than make learning to listen something that is learned slowly over the course of the group, it seems appropriate to do a little direct teaching. Group members will be required to work in pairs and small groups as well as in the whole group, so it is particularly necessary that they can be relied upon to listen to each other. More than one opportunity is given in the early days of the group for learning this skill.

Hopes and fears

It is inevitable that there will be considerable anxieties for those attending the first meeting of the group. This may be particularly so for our group members because they will all have failed previous treatments for their obesity. Yet their very presence in the group indicates that they have some hope of a better outcome. It is better that these anxieties are openly expressed at the very beginning of the group, so that they do not create obstacles to participation in the group (Hodge, 1997; Benson, 2001).

Chapter 6
Training for Leading a Treatment Group

Training of the group leaders

As you will have understood by now, the programme we have devised is capable of arousing strong reactions in the participants. We feel that this is appropriate. It seems clear that food and eating are extremely powerful subjects for most people and carry with them a wealth of association and meaning. If we want people to change their eating behaviour it seems extremely likely that strong feelings will be aroused. You, as group leader, must be competent to deal with a group of women who are being put in touch with memories and associations that may well be difficult.

We consider that if you are taking on the leadership of one of these groups you must, at a minimum, have counselling training and experience of running groups. Many counsellors are trained in specific theoretical approaches to counselling, e.g. CBT, person centred, psychodynamic. As we have already explained this programme draws on a wide range of approaches. If you feel uneasy about combining different approaches or if you feel a semi-structured group is difficult for you, you should not undertake the running of one of these groups. The group programme will demand from you an openness to a range of theoretical and methodological approaches.

However, we think it is also very important that you should have trained specifically to conduct this programme. As we have already discussed, most obese women have had experience of weight loss interventions because of an apparent failure of empathy on the part of those conducting them. Hoppe and Ogden (1997) found, for example, that slender nurses were likely to blame obese patients for their weight. Training needs to be particularly concerned with getting potential group leaders to review the history of their own relationship with food and related themes such as their relationship with their body, self-esteem, their internal voice, etc. We think that working with vulnerable group members without having addressed these issues in your own life is likely to limit severely your capacity to run the group. In our experience these themes are very important for most women and addressing them in one's own life increases and develops empathy for group members.

Training should involve you in working through the programme and both discussing how it operates and taking part in a selection of the exercises yourself. We think there is no substitute for experiencing just how profound the relationship with food and our bodies can be. If you feel unwilling to put yourself through this sort of training programme, you might ask yourself whether it is ethical to offer a group a treatment which you are not willing to undergo yourself. Our motto is, 'If you can't take it, don't dish it out', or as Benson (2001) says more elegantly 'Never take a group or its members into any experience you would not be prepared to go into yourself' (p. 51).

We also think that it is important that you are equipped for the management of very powerful feelings in the group. There is no merit whatever in having group members retraumatised and, besides, the effect is likely to be that they leave the group. The groups are deliberately recruited from women who have difficult histories; it is very likely that this will become apparent during the life of the group. Ideally you should have training in the management of post-traumatic stress. Furthermore, you should ensure that you have appropriate supervision for this work. It is strenuous to lead a group of this nature and you need support.

Men as group leaders

As discussed previously this programme is in the process of being researched with women. Similarly all group leaders so far have been women. The rationale for female group leaders has been that women's experience of food and nurturing and their bodies is very different to male experience. Since one of our primary goals has been to develop empathy in our group leaders it has seemed more appropriate to train women. However, we recognise that there are men within the therapeutic world who are more than capable of empathic understanding. McKisack and Waller (1997) found no advantage attached to the gender of the therapist in groups for bulimics. We suspect that men's relationship with alcohol may have more commonalities with women's relationship with food than with men's relationship with food, but that may enable them to empathise with women. We have also noticed that many of the women in our groups have exceedingly difficult histories of relationships with men and we wonder how easy it would be for a man to run a group in these circumstances. We hope that men who would like to run one of these programmes will prepare themselves appropriately to do so and let us know about their experience.

The University of Hertfordshire runs training courses totalling 30 hours for this programme and also offers supervision. If you contact us at j.buckroyd@herts.ac.uk or s.m.rother@herts.ac.uk we can give you details.

PART II

The Programme

Introduction to the Programme

The protocol is intended as a guide but it is not meant to be followed like a knitting pattern. It is impossible to predict how a group will react to the experience and it is important for you as group leader to feel that you have the authority to vary the programme if circumstances demand. In general you are likely to find that you have more material than you can use and that discussions take longer than allowed for in the protocol. As long as you feel that the discussion is useful, then that is fine. You may even find that you want to omit whole exercises. That is also fine, as long as you feel that the essential themes of the group are being addressed.

The time splits are a guide, not a rule. But with a largish number of people, everything takes a long time, so take care not to arrive at the conclusion of each session without time for a proper ending. Participants often have stressful and difficult lives, so it's only fair that they leave feeling reasonably calm and collected.

Session 1

Time split

- Introductions and boundary setting   25 minutes
- Hopes and fears / outline programme   35 minutes
- Listening exercise   25 minutes
- Sharing information   25 minutes
- Ending   10 minutes

Aims and objectives

- To begin to establish the group as a protected space within which emotional exploration and sharing is possible.

The necessary preliminary is the housekeeping and setting of boundaries:

- Venue - toilets - escape routes, etc.
- 36-week group over a calendar year – agree dates if not already established.
- Weekly meetings of 2 hours.
- Emphasis on importance of attendance.
- Notification of Absence – a system devised by each group leader to allow participants to contact the group leader. (Give out written details.)
- Contacting group members. (Circulate a list of names and ask all members to indicate how they wish to be contacted, e.g. letter, e-mail, telephone, mobile, text.)
- Notebook, envelope file and pen given out, named if possible.
- Use labels for names.
- Group confidentiality statement: give out and get it signed and returned (see Appendix 1).
- Rules for behaviour, i.e. no harming themselves or others or damaging the environment.

Introductory exercise

Suggest they say their name and one thing about themselves or use some other very simple introductory device.

Hopes and fears

This exercise allows for the expression of the inevitable feelings that will have been aroused before the group even begins. The logic of getting them into the open is that they are less likely to be disruptive once expressed. As group leader you may also find that there are some misapprehensions about what is going to happen which you will then have the opportunity to correct. It may also be appropriate to use this opportunity to acknowledge the reality that the group will all be looking at each other and deciding who is the fattest or thinnest. It may be an early opportunity to say something about acceptance of difference.

Hopes

- To lose weight and sustain the weight loss
- To be healthy
- Finding the missing part of myself
- To understand myself better
- To feel confident and have better self-esteem
- To feel worthy and less self loathing
- To stop blaming myself
- To grow up
- To understand my relationship with food
- To address reasons for overeating
- To learn another way to manage emotions
- Not to pass habits on to my children
- To develop a different lifestyle
- To make a permanent change
- To meet some similar sized women
- To get some support and make friends

Fears

- What I might discover
- Failing
- Change
- That the group will not work
- The other people in the group
- The commitment
- My emotions might get out of control
- Leaving the session in a state
- Getting bigger instead of smaller
- Looking better
- Not being wanted
- Not sustaining the weight loss

You could begin the exercise by getting them to work individually using their new notebooks and then get them to divide into small groups (3 or 4) to draw up a list together. You could supply them with a large sheet of paper to do this. These sheets could then be put on the wall or the floor for all to look at. Or you could do a collective list, with you as scribe for the whole group. (**Keep this data.**)

You are the only one who knows in any detail what is actually on the menu, so you need to use this first meeting as the opportunity to give them an outline of what the values of the group are, what we are trying to accomplish and what the next 36 meetings are going to involve. Give them the outline (Appendix 2). Give some time for reactions and discussion.

Listening exercise

Explain to the group that they will be learning to listen very carefully to each other in a way that people do not normally do. This skill needs to be learned and practised. Explain the basic principles of eye contact, body posture, not interrupting, etc., and then suggest that they work in pairs, sharing with each other how they use food. Get them to reflect on how they felt about disclosing, how well they felt they were listened to, and whether there is anything they need to remember for listening in the future. You can return to the issue of listening over the first few weeks, whenever they work in pairs or small groups. It is also something that you can flag up when they are working in the whole group, particularly if sub-conversations are going on.

Sharing information

The main business for the rest of this first session is to do an exercise on sharing information with others. This work will be continued in the next session, so this is just the first attempt. These women have probably no notion of sharing information about themselves in this way so there needs to be an introduction to the whole concept of confidentiality to the pair, responsibility as to how much they choose to say, etc.

You could begin by reminding them that earlier in the session they signed a group confidentiality agreement. You can now begin to discuss its meaning and implications. You can also use the prior discussions and information to talk about how they think they will feel about talking about themselves to other people. They have just had a small experience in the listening exercise; ask them whether this is something they do with friends; what their experience is of sharing, and possibly betrayal, of confidences. You should mention that trust is something that is earned and that it will take time for it to develop between other group members and with you. You have time to discuss these issues fairly fully.

Ending

Try and keep 10 minutes at least for this. You have given group members a very rich and powerful experience, which may even have felt quite overwhelming. Try to do a bit of debriefing, calming, sending on their way.

Homework

- For this first session the homework should be nothing more demanding than inviting them to think about what has been said during the session and how it might apply to them

Session 2

Time split

- Review   10 minutes
- Weightline / lifeline exercise   25 minutes
- Motivational enhancement   30 minutes
- Food monitoring   45 minutes
- Ending   10 minutes

Aims and objectives

- Review the first session.
- To facilitate the group in exploring whether there is a connection between their weight gains and losses and food use and their emotional lives.
- Enhance motivation for change.
- Introduce monitoring sheets.

Review First Session

Try to facilitate as open a discussion as possible on how group members experienced the first session. Bearing in mind what they said in the exercise on hopes and fears, try to identify the disappointments as well as the satisfactions. Try also to get them to be patient and give the group a decent chance. This second session is crucial. If they feel reasonably satisfied after two sessions there is a very good chance they will stay the course.

Weightline/lifeline exercise

Aim: To explore the relationship between participants' emotional history and their weight in order to introduce the concept that their food use may be partly driven by feelings and emotional experience.

Ask participants to:

- Draw a line in their new notebooks and plot on it weight gains and losses as far back as they can remember.
- Plot against that line what was going on in their lives at those particular times.
- Work together in pairs to discuss/share what has been said.
- Bring this together by sharing in the whole group.

Sometimes this exercise is very powerful, but at the very least it usually provides quite a bit of insight. In our experience most people connect life events and eating behaviour.

Weightline

Weight gain was associated with loss

- *Death of a Nan*
- *Best friend moves away*
- *Son leaves home*
- *Divorce*
- *Death of a parent*
- *Loneliness*

Weight loss

- *I was in love and got everything I needed from the relationship. I didn't need food*
- *When my mother finally died I was so relieved the weight just dropped off me*

Motivational enhancement

Prochaska et al. (1992) spent their working lives investigating the processes involved in change. They felt that if people were not ready for change, then efforts to help them to change were a waste of time. Their work has been used to improve motivation. This approach has been used a lot in drug and alcohol services to allocate resources appropriately. Schmidt and Treasure (1997) are convinced that it is equally vital in working with eating disorders. Their major point is that unless the ambivalence about change is addressed, resistance will undermine the process and progress will be sabotaged. This point of view works well from a psychodynamic perspective, which acknowledges different and interacting parts of the self. This session begins the process of getting participants to acknowledge their ambivalence and take responsibility for it, so that they do not project it on to the group.

Draw the process of change diagram on the flip chart and/or hand out the diagram (see Appendix 3). Remember that one of the criteria for inclusion in the group was readiness to take action about weight, and also that all participants have had their motivation tested by being required to attend for an interview. Explain the wheel and get people to identify where they are on it. They will probably be on the cusp of preparation/action. You can ask them if they can identify being at other points at other times in their lives – thus making the point that we move round the circle. Point out that at any stage there is the potential for both progression and regression.

Then try to introduce the idea that we have different voices inside us, some for change and progress and some not. Get group members to identify in their notebooks their own reasons for changing and not changing. Share this information in the whole group, perhaps by a list on the flip chart. (**Keep this data.**)

> - It's so hard to know where to put myself in relation to change. With my thinking part I'm all ready to go and I know all the good reasons why I should lose weight. But in my feelings it's so different. My feelings get in the way of doing what I know I should. If I change who will I be?
> - Although I want to lose weight I'm frightened to. If I'm thin and attractive I'm afraid men will give me too much attention.

Try to talk about how we can all expect to feel resistance and ambivalence about change at some points. Heinz Kohut (1984) thought that many people had very little understanding of how other people think and experience the world. We are apt to suppose that our way of going on is entirely unique. In fact it is useful for us to understand that there are vast commonalities in the way human beings operate. Those who have had difficult beginnings are often least aware of these common denominators. In this group we have a number of women who share a problem. It is extremely likely that they will all have had experience of wanting and not wanting to change. Kohut's recommendation was that behaviour should, where possible, be normalised. 'Yes, of course you will feel resistant. It makes perfect sense that you would feel that way.' This, he thought, enabled people to feel that they belonged to the human race and were not strange or freakish.

Introducing monitoring

Follow this by introducing the idea of monitoring. This will very likely produce instant resistance because members will assume that you are asking them to keep a food diary. This is a common device in dieting circles and is often experienced as shaming. Talk about how you are not interested at this point so much in **what** they eat, but how their eating relates to the rest of their lives. Give out the sheets (see Appendix 4) and let them have a look at them. You will note that they are not asked to describe what they ate although, in the responses that some of our participants made (see below), you will see that they assumed that we wanted them to keep a record of what they ate. Make sure that they are all crystal clear about what they are being asked to do. Point out how the sheet asks them to relate their eating behaviour to the time of day, circumstance and mood. It also asks them whether they ate more than they wanted and what their hunger and satisfaction states were before and after. Tell them that you are interested in the patterns that they may be able to identify. Get them to practise using the sheet by filling in what they did yesterday. This may or may not produce insight, but will at least show them how to use the sheet. Ask them to fill in one sheet for each day until the next group meeting. Give them as much time as you can to express their responses to the prospect of this task. This is the first significant demand on them; it's important that they take on the challenge of doing some work.

- I don't want to do this.
- It's just like Weight Watchers.
- It makes me eat more when I have to keep a record like this.
- It's so boring.
- Well I'm certainly not going to make a list of what I eat. You would be disgusted and it would make me feel worse.

You should note at this point that participants may not yet be sufficiently aware of how they use food for emotional regulation to be able to use the monitoring sheets to identify the link between feelings and eating behaviour. As you progress through the next few sessions their awareness should increase; however, you should keep the option open to continue using these sheets or to reintroduce them later in the programme.

Ending

Be sure to leave at least 5–10 minutes for ending. Once again they have had a rich experience, probably very unlike any previous experience. Give them a little time to debrief and collect themselves before they leave.

Homework

- Complete monitoring sheets.

Session 3

Time split

- Review   30 minutes
- Strategies for managing impulses
      to overeat   20 minutes
- Names for feelings   15 minutes
- Managing feelings   40 minutes
- Ending   15 minutes

Aims and objectives

- Review Session 2, especially completion of monitoring sheets.
- Explore cognitive behavioural strategies for managing overeating.
- Begin to investigate feelings and how they are expressed.
- Begin learning about management of feelings.

Review

The main thing to review in this session is members' experience of filling in the monitoring sheets. Try getting them to discuss it in small groups first. Then do a brainstorming on the flip chart using these questions to shape the discussion

- How have they managed it?
- How have they felt about it?
- How has their eating behaviour been?
- What have they learned?

- *I couldn't bear to do it. I left the monitoring sheets in the boot of the car.*
- *I just can't identify what I'm feeling; I don't know. I just feel numb.*
- *I know what my overeating is about. It is about comfort and reward.*
- *I know why I eat. I'm resentful and bored.*
- *I know that I eat before I get hungry. I don't want to feel that feeling of being hungry and empty.*
- *It's the first time I've really recognised that I eat when I'm not hungry.*
- *I feel so ashamed when I see that I eat because of what I'm feeling and not because I'm hungry.*
- *I eat in the evening; my husband sits upstairs with the computer and I feel lonely.*
- *I eat to give myself affection; I love myself by giving myself food to fill up the void. I've been waiting for years for someone to come along and love me so that I can be thin again.*

For some people there will be an issue about hiding the monitoring sheets from others in their household. Don't be surprised if compliance has been poor. The job is tedious at best and shaming at worst. In the nicest possible way, try to address poor compliance by going back to ambivalence about change. You might want to get them to make a list of why they want to fill in the sheets and why they don't want to. Emphasise what has been learned. Give out more monitoring sheets for the coming week.

Strategies for managing overeating

This sort of thing is what some members really want and will be looking for. Start to identify who at this stage finds cognitive work more helpful and who finds emotional work more useful.

There are two basic approaches to managing behaviour: one is to find a distraction, alternative or substitute behaviour; the other is to address the problem that the behaviour is trying to resolve. On this occasion we are only dealing with the first approach.

You could do this via a brainstorming exercise. Get them to provide a scenario or two that seem typical, e.g. sitting down in front of the TV and starting to snack; getting in from work and bingeing.

- As soon as I get in after work I take the dog for a walk. That helps me not start to eat straight away.
- I'm scared of picking when I'm making the dinner. I try and put the radio on so that I have something else to think about.
- I just never have biscuits or chocolates in the house. I know I won't be strong enough to resist them. If people give me things like that I give them away to other people.
- I think I'm bored watching television and that's why I eat so I've taken up knitting at the same time which keeps my hands busy.
- Magazines always tell you to have a bath with nice oils and things.
- If I feel like raiding the fridge I try to phone my friend instead but it's so disappointing if she's not there. Then I have a real binge.

Ask them if they have ever been able to stop or avoid the behaviour. What strategies worked? Usually the answer is a variation on 'doing something else or avoiding the situation'. You can make suggestions but try to get them to recognise that they have already identified their own resources on some previous occasions. This is one of the strategies for solution focused therapy (Jacob, 2001) – to identify solutions previously employed and support the client in trying them again. The idea of course is empowerment. This week particularly, be careful not to overrun the time on this first part. If you take a bit less time, that is fine.

Names for feelings

Some people within the group are certain to be alexithymic (people who have no words for feelings). The women in the group will know words such as disappointed or happy, they will have read them in books and seen them on the television, but to be able to use them in a meaningful way is altogether something else. To be able to recognise the physical syndrome that means anxious or disappointed or angry is a skill that needs to be learned. You want them to begin to be able to use words to describe internal feelings. With many compulsive eaters, and people with eating disorders in general, the process where a feeling is experienced, named and then acted on is conflated. The person will go from a feeling, which never gets into consciousness, to a response to it that is physical. The women within the group are not saying "I feel anxious so I am going to eat a chocolate biscuit". They are anxious but do not know they are anxious. They only know that they are eating a chocolate biscuit.

Brainstorm words for feelings using a flip chart. Ask participants to tell you the names of feelings and try to collect a page full. This gives the participants a starting point with a basis of names of feelings. (The Mr Men books are quite useful in the way the titles describe people and may also be another helpful means of naming feelings for the group members.)

Follow up the brainstorming by getting them to write a list in their books of feelings that they are familiar with, from the list on the board. You may be surprised how short the list is. Get them into pairs or small groups to give examples of when they feel those feelings.

- I know about the sorts of feelings like pain or tired or, sometimes, hungry but I don't know about the other sorts.
- The feeling I know best is guilty.
- I don't do feelings.
- I just feel numb. I've no idea what I feel.
- I think I miss out anger and fly into an uncontrollable rage like my father used to.
- I feel stupid a lot of the time.
- I feel anxious. I wish I didn't.

Managing feelings

One of the basic tools that you are going to supply is an understanding of how feelings can be managed and what has happened to a person who finds them too difficult to manage. One bit of feed-back from the very first hopes and fears exercise (page 54) includes two statements that indicate how frightening feelings can be to this client group. There were two fears expressed: "My emotions might get out of control" and "Leaving the session in a state". These anxieties are probably common to the group so you are going to begin by describing how feelings are regulated and managed in a good situation and what happens in a bad situation (see Appendix 5). You will see that Appendix 5 is a simplified version of the model that was described on page 19–22. Use your own judgement about how much complexity to include. The essential point you are trying to make is that affect regulation is a skill that fortunate people learn in early childhood and have available to them thereafter. Less fortunate people are more liable to be overwhelmed by their feelings. You can also explain how a person with reasonably good affect management skills can be overwhelmed by unusual trauma. Trail the prospect that you will be teaching them how to enhance affect management skills or install them for the first time if they didn't get them early on.

Ending

Use the ending to focus them on tasks for the next week: to continue with monitoring; to develop strategies for managing overeating; and to work on being more aware of their feelings. Suggest that they think about the material on affect regulation. Give time for discussion about how it feels to have these tasks to perform.

Homework

- As in Ending above.

Session 4

Time split

- Review   30 minutes
- Reviewing motivation   30 minutes
- Feelings in the family   20 minutes
- Managing feelings   30 minutes
- Ending   10 minutes

Aims and objectives

- To review the last session.
- To revisit motivation and strategies for managing overeating.
- To continue work on the expression of feelings.
- To continue work on affect management.

Review

This week the review needs to cover both the keeping of monitoring sheets and reactions to the exercise on feelings. I suggest you start with the monitoring. You will be revisiting ambivalence and motivation later this session, so concentrate at this point on what they can see from the monitoring. Are they able to identify patterns in their overeating? Are they becoming more aware of how their mood affects their eating behaviour? This is an opportunity for you to see who is working in the group so far, and who is waiting for a miracle and will lead you directly to the next exercise.

Leave discussion on the expression and management of feelings to later in the session.

Reviewing motivation

Ask them to get out their handouts with the diagram of the change process on it and ask them where they are now, compared with where they were two weeks ago. Have some spares with you for those who have lost their copy (note who they are).

- I think I've slipped back. I think I've gone back to preparation
- I thought I was really keen to get on with sorting all this out but it's harder than I thought
- I feel pleased it's the first time in a long time that I've actually managed to do anything for myself
- I think it's really hard to accept that it's all down to me and that I'm the one that has to do something. I think I've been waiting for a miracle

Ask them about the monitoring as an exercise and how they feel about it. Recognise that it is very tedious, but be alive to more substantial objections. Hand out more monitoring sheets, either now or later, if it feels more appropriate.

- I see now how many food snacks of sugar I eat and how few meals I eat in a week.
- I have done so many diets but I don't know how to eat properly.
- I realise I eat before I get hungry. I panic if I feel hungry. I will eat anything and everything until I feel sick.
- I take food with me everywhere I go just in case I'm held up and don't get home in time. I'm really scared of being hungry and having no food.

Then ask how they managed with the strategies for avoiding overeating. How successful were they; are there any additions to be made to the list?

Then ask them about the group and their feelings about it. Try to address all the negative things. We would guess that already some will be disappointed that they haven't had diet sheets and that it is not already fixing them and their weight. Ask them how long it has taken them to get to the size they are and how many times they have tried to lose weight before. Try to get them to see that they are attempting something different and more permanent this time, which will take longer.

- I'm such a perfectionist I daren't start to change anything in case I fail.
- I'm going to ask for a stomach staple. This talking stuff isn't working.
- It's wonderful being among a group of people who've experienced the same difficulties as I have.

The group dynamic will also have started to develop by this time. Give some thought as to whether you need to intervene in it. Remember, this is not a conventional therapy group in which you would wait for the group to deal with any problems. Eventually you may get to that point, but that is not what the priority is at the moment. Our experience suggests that you need to notice behaviour that is significantly disruptive, e.g. someone who monopolises the time, or members who talk to each other during the proceedings. You also need to look out for those who are unduly silent. People who don't disclose or contribute eventually become like voyeurs and a focus for group hostility. Try to encourage universal participation.

Feelings in the family

Preface this exercise with a review of last week's exercise on investigating feelings and then progress to Feelings in the Family. This exercise uses a family systems approach showing that the possible feelings in the family are divided up. This seems to be extremely common, particularly so in dysfunctional families. It is a very well-functioning family where everybody can feel everything.

Ask participants to work individually and, using the list of feelings from last week that you put on the flip chart, write down:

- Which feelings from this list were felt and expressed in their family?
- Who felt them?
- Which feelings do they recognise and which feelings were they allowed to have in their families?

Suggest drawing a little diagram of the people in their family and to make a list beside these people of the feelings that each of them had. You might want to go back to the food in the family exercise and get them to think about who felt what in that situation.

Ask participants to give an example of how these feelings were expressed in their family, e.g. father became silent when angry; mother cried when disappointed; sister slammed doors when angry; self ate packet of biscuits when unhappy.

- My father was always angry so I never dared to be.
- When my mother was shouted at by my father she would be unkind and shout at me. I used to go to my room and punch the wall and then sob for hours.
- I wasn't allowed to show any difficult feelings. I just had to be good and quiet and get on with it.
- Looking back, I was scared a lot of the time so I just kept out of the way.
- When my Dad was away we all used to relax and my Mum would produce a wholesome meal and we would take comfort in eating.

Ask participants to get into pairs and discuss this with their partner. Maybe remind them of listening skills.

More on managing feelings

This exercise builds on what you did last week, exploring how children learn to manage feelings. Ask them what they thought in relation to the exercise since last week. Expect to hear that plenty of them had mothers who could not help with affect management. Then explain that there are strategies they can learn, now as adults, which will compensate, at least a bit, for what they didn't get as children and go on to teach them the first one, creating a container for feelings.

Participants are asked to imagine a container which will hold all their unpleasant or disturbing experience. This container has a valve which allows further material to be inserted into it but also allows material to be released from it in as small a quantity as the participant wishes and only when she permits. Participants should be asked how much of their difficult material they have managed to seal in the container and should be encouraged to continue visualisation until all material is safely contained. They may call on others (God or any other ally) to help them with this process. This process empowers the participant by enabling them to remove disturbing material from consciousness at will, but also gives a way of enabling the work of the group to go on so that it is not deflected by too much trauma. Test the process by asking how much of their disturbing material they think is still outside the container and ask them what help they need to ensure that it is all put safely away. Get them to visualise whatever help they need.

Explain that this strategy can be used by them at any point when they feel that their feelings are too much for them and suggest that they practise during the week.

Ending

Use the ending to focus them on the tasks for the next week: to continue with monitoring and to work on their awareness of their own feelings and those of other people. Ask them to think about the container strategy and see if they can find useful moments to use it. In addition, ask them to talk to another group member about their experience in the group this week. Remind them that they are to talk about their own experience and not gossip about other people. (Get them to write these tasks in their notebook if they think they won't remember.)

Homework

- Continue with monitoring.
- Work on awareness of feelings.
- Practice putting feelings in a container.
- Talk to one other person in the group about their experience in the group.

Session 5

Time split

- Review   20 minutes
- Buddying   30 minutes
- Meal planning   30 minutes
- More on managing feelings   30 minutes
- Ending   10 minutes

Aims and objectives

- Review of monitoring and last week.
- Preliminary discussion on buddying.
- Introduction of meal planning.
- Further work on managing feelings.

Review

By this time, five weeks in, you should be seeing signs of change and a development of insight and understanding. The feeling of the group should be becoming stronger and more cohesive. It might be about now that you might challenge those who don't appear to be working and try to discover what is going on. Use the review of monitoring to assess this.

Talk about the monitoring. They have now done it four times. What have they learned about the patterns of their food use? You might want to get them to discuss in small groups. Acknowledge the difficulties of doing it. By this time we would expect them to be starting to understand their behaviour better. That may not mean that their behaviour has changed very much yet (although we would expect some change) but it should mean that their attitudes to their overeating are changing.

Ask about feelings and their awareness of them after last week and how they managed using the idea of a container for feelings. Then ask them how they got on with telling others what is going on for them, which will lead you neatly to the next exercise.

Buddying

Lots of books on eating disorders and related subjects (dieting, etc.) recommend that participants find someone who can act as their buddy. Last week the group members were asked to contact one other group member to talk to about what has been going on for them in the group. Some will have done this; some will not. It is likely that all group members will have a history of using food instead of people. Begin this exercise by asking them if they think it might be true that they use food instead of people to manage their emotional lives. Get them to talk about what they use food for and why they don't use people. Suggest to them that it is very ordinary for all of us to use other people to help us through life's difficulties. Maybe there are special reasons why they don't. Have they been let down by those they could reasonably expect to help them? Have they lost hope that other people will offer them anything if they are in difficulties?

How could a buddy help them?

Do a group exercise drawing up the qualities of a buddy, e.g. someone who can listen, doesn't judge, will be supportive, etc. Then ask them if they think that some people in the group could have that function for them. Would there be an advantage in having small support groups within the group? In either case would it be an advantage to have a confidentiality agreement? What should be in it? What about including agreements about how a time to phone is to be negotiated, e.g. what happens if one phones and the other person is too busy to talk? If it seems appropriate, draw up an agreement. Ask them if they want it typed, etc., and if so, is there someone in the group who will do it? Having people select others in the group is difficult because of the whole business of rejection. In order to avoid that, you might want to suggest that they form themselves into little cells of 3 or 4. Leave the discussion here and suggest that people think about it during the week and you return to the whole subject next week.

> **N.B:** The successful introduction of buddying depends on a degree of trust having been established in the group. if you feel that it is too soon for this step, delay it until you feel it is right.

Meal planning

Explain that we are stopping one kind of monitoring but going on to another. There is a consensus that many overweight people have chaotic eating patterns. If these can be regularised as a preliminary to work on food choices, it will help. Secondly, you should explain to them that binges are often set up by attempts to cut back after previous binges. One binge sets up the next. If they can maintain regular eating, despite the binges, it will help to prevent bingeing. Thirdly, many overeaters panic if they feel that they need food. If their intake is already planned, so that they know they are 'allowed' to eat at fixed times, it can both manage the panic and prevent overeating. Those who eat too much at mealtimes and don't otherwise binge, should be encouraged to use the planning to see that if they are eating more frequently, they may not need to 'binge' at mealtimes. By this time you should have a feel for how they use food and can stress whatever seems appropriate.

- I've never planned a meal in my life; I just go and look and see what's in the fridge.
- I'm not going to do this. I've spent my whole life being told what to do.
- I can't manage this; there's too much going on in my life. I can't concentrate on doing this as well.
- Planning a meal? Are you joking? In my family you just grab what you can when you can.
- Maybe it will help if I can see that I am going to have lots of chances to eat during the day.
- I'm afraid I'll make lovely plans and just continue the way I do now.

Give out the food planning sheets (see Appendix 6). Tell them that at this point it is more important that they eat regularly than that they alter what they eat. If they seem to want to restrict, tell them that we will be coming on to discuss food choices later. As a preliminary, get them to write down the pattern of their eating the previous day. Lots of them will probably be skipping breakfast or eating all day long or eating one huge amount in the evening. Watch out for those who claim to be doing none of these things – how did they get to be so big then? Then get them to plan their food for the rest of this day and/or tomorrow. How does it feel? Check up on the ambivalence. What are the feelings and reasons against doing it? Ask them to plan for each day for the next week as their homework and to note how they feel.

More on managing feelings

It is possible that difficult emotions have been aroused at this point so it is a good moment to continue with strategies for managing feelings. Group members are asked to identify a safe place. This will be a place known or imagined where she cannot be harmed. One group member chose her grandmother's bed as her safe place. She remembered it as a soft, warm, clean haven where she could snuggle under the duvet. At the same time group members are asked to notice how they feel in their bodies when they are in this safe place. This strategy of remembering how it feels to be in a safe place and the identification of a safe place can both be used when participants feel that a situation may overwhelm them.

Ending

This session has covered a wide range of material and has introduced the difficult concepts of buddying and meal planning. You have provided them with another skill for affect management but it is possible that the whole session has been quite powerful. Try to soothe and calm them. Congratulate them on all the hard work they are doing.

Homework

- Complete meal planning sheets. Think about what has been said about the possibility of buddying. Practise using the safe place strategy.

Session 6

Time split	
• Review	15 minutes
• Buddying	15 minutes
• More on managing feelings	20 minutes
• Use of food in your family	55 minutes
• Ending	15 minutes

Aims and objectives

- Review meal planning and feelings in family from last week.
- Continue with buddying.
- Continue with managing feelings.
- Explore food use in the family of origin.

Review

Start with the buddying. Find out what they've done, if anything – how it felt, did it help, etc. For those who haven't yet done anything, try to discover the ambivalence. Do an exercise on for and against buddying if necessary. Does anything need to be followed up about the confidentiality agreement? How have they used the strategies for managing feelings? Have they any questions?

Discuss how they managed with the meal planning. Ask them to get out the meal planning sheets if they have them with them. How difficult was it to do this? Was there any relief in having a structure for eating? Did it affect what they ate or how much they ate? Was there anybody for whom the meal planning felt unhelpful? Tell them that there is good evidence to suggest meal planning helps avoid bingeing and overeating. Ask them to continue with it.

Buddying

Last week all the preliminary work for setting up a buddying system was completed. Group members were asked to go away and think about how they felt about such a system and to contact one other group member to discuss it. Use this time for as thorough a discussion as you can elicit of the pros and cons. Remember, this is a group of people who are likely to have real problems with trust and little experience of using others for management of their feelings. Unless there is very fierce resistance, get agreement that cell members contact at least one other in the coming week. Ask them to compile a list of contact details for their cell. The previous weeks in which they have been asked to do that without a formal system being set up should help them. The power of the last exercise this week is considerable and it would be very desirable for them to use each other to contain it during the following week.

More on managing feelings

This is the third and, so far, most important strategy for managing feelings. It is usually referred to as grounding. The theory is that when difficult memories and feelings are aroused, a person is liable to lose the sense of herself in the present with her adult competence and get transported into a child part relating to the memory or feeling. If this happens the original trauma can be repeated so that instead of finding that the memories are resolved or made more bearable, they are merely strengthened by being re-experienced. One strategy to prevent that happening is to ensure that the adult self is present in the scenario and to do that the person needs to be taught how to stay 'grounded' in the present. There are a number of strategies for doing this. Here we will only mention two. If you know or learn others that you prefer, feel free to use them. Each participant is asked to imagine a cord which fixes her to the earth and holds her in the present and grounded. When she feels that her feelings may overwhelm her she can visualise the grounding cord fixing her to the earth and the present. An alternative image is to ask the participant to press her feet flat on the ground and feel her muscles holding her strongly. At the same time the participant is asked to notice the physical feeling in her body of being grounded and present. The idea is to bring the person back to the present from the experience of the trauma or, alternatively, to place the adult self there in the trauma with the child. These strategies can be used by the participants at any time but you can use them in the sessions with participants that you can see are being overwhelmed. Strategies such as asking the person to make eye contact and say her name will also be useful in interrupting an experience of trauma. Be prepared to use this strategy in the next exercise.

Use of food in the participants' family or childhood scenario

This is a powerful exercise, likely to arouse strong feelings in some people. It is also relatively early in the life of the group, which may therefore not yet feel a very strong container for feelings. Make sure that you leave plenty of time for it and for debriefing thereafter. Encourage participants to use the strategies for managing feelings which you have been teaching them. If any one of them gets overwhelmed (as is not uncommon) work with her using the grounding exercise to bring her back to the present and assure her that she is no longer a child in that situation and that it can no longer harm her.

The exercise will enable participants to start to think about their family of origin and also their current family in terms of food use in order to illustrate that food use is at least, in part, learned within the family and a response to the family dynamic. You may want to suggest that those who know their experience was difficult see the memory as a video that can be paused or stopped if necessary.

N.B: At this point you need to indicate that you are aware that not everyone grows up in a conventional family setting. Families are often disrupted – blended families, fostering, in care, etc. Some children are made responsible for feeding themselves and sometimes others. Make sure you talk in a way that includes these possibilities.

Ask participants to:

- Think about themselves as a child at a time when they can remember a fair bit about what went on, preferably before age 11.
- Think about themselves at an age when they can remember where they were living and, specifically, the room in which their family (or those they were living with) ate its meals. (If participants say they can't remember anything, let them choose whatever time is the earliest they can remember.)
- Draw a diagram of the room in which the meals were taken, putting in the furniture, the television, the dog and any other important things that were there.
- Label the people.

Now ask them to answer the following questions:

1. In your situation, who cooked the food or made the meals?
2. What did that person feel about those jobs and in what kind of spirit did they approach them?

    —Did they like them?
    —Did they resent them?
    —Did they feel that that was what they **wanted** to do or what they **had** to do?

3. Who was the food in the family prepared for? (Give an illustration; make it up if necessary – "I know a family where the food is made for the father. It's what he wants and likes that decides what they eat. If he isn't there they eat completely different food)." Who was the important eater?

    —Was it the children?
    —Was it one of the adults?

4. What do you think the emotional purpose of mealtimes was in your situation?

    - What was supposed to happen there?
    - What was not supposed to happen?
    - Was it an opportunity for everybody to quarrel?
    - Was it an opportunity for the parents to be evil tempered with each other?
    - Was it an opportunity to bully the children?
    - Was it an opportunity to have a nice time together and share the events of the day?
    - Was it an opportunity to say nothing, or to make sure that nothing was said, e.g. by having the television on?

5. Look at your diagram of the room and think about each person in turn.

   - What might each person be saying and to whom?
   - What would be said to you, and what would you say, if anything?
   - Write those things on the diagram.

6. What was your feeling memory of these occasions?

   - What sort of an occasion was it for you?
   - What sorts of things went on that you remember?

7. When you think about all of this – do you think that what went on at mealtimes was a picture of what went on in the family as a whole?

   - Do you think it is an illustration of the relationships in the family?
   - Was that how your family behaved generally?

8. Do you think you had any power?
9. Who did have the power?

Take no more than 25 minutes for these questions. Give participants a copy of the questions as a reminder (see Appendix 7). Ask them to get into groups of three and discuss their answers, taking about half an hour, that is, 10 minutes for each person. Remind them to share the time evenly. This might be a moment to remind them of listening skills. Get one person in each group to keep the time.

Take at least 15 minutes for a more general discussion in the whole group, including:

- How members felt doing the exercise?
- What kind of memories it raised for them?
- Asking them to name the feelings.
- Asking them how they reacted to what other people said?
- Asking them what they learned about themselves and whether they can see any connection with their present behaviour?

You should be aware that this exercise often produces very strong feelings among group members. Be prepared to use the exercises for managing feelings that you have been teaching them. People often cry and are surprised by the ease with which memories and feelings are recovered. Remember that group members are very likely to be new to this kind of reflection and taken by surprise by the strength of their feelings. On the other hand, there may be people who cannot remember much, if anything, about their childhood.

You want them to come back next week so make sure this experience is contained and that the courage of group members is validated. Be sure to include some material about how this exercise might make them change things in the present.

- At meal times there was only me and my mother. I was frightened of her then just as I was the rest of the time. I didn't know when she'd start to hit me.
- My mother was very thin. She stayed in the kitchen feeding everybody else but she couldn't feed herself.
- When I was just 12 years old I took a banana from the fruit bowl with out asking permission. I wasn't allowed to take food without asking. My father flew in to a rage because of my disobedience. He forced me to eat the whole bunch of bananas very quickly one after another. I couldn't hardly breathe.
- Mealtimes had to be silent and I hated them.
- My mother gave me love but it came in food parcels.
- It's my mum's fault that I eat like I do. She never believed I was hungry and if she had just let me have one biscuit when I came home from school I wouldn't need to eat the whole tin now.

Ending

This has been the most powerful exercise so far. Take 15 minutes for debriefing. This would be a good occasion for using a de-roling exercise. This is another strategy for managing feelings. You could ask them all to stand up saying their name, age and situation, e.g. I was a small child in a family. I am now a grown woman. I am 42 years old. I am living with a partner with two children and my name is Gloria. I have the power to make choices in my life.

Leave them feeling that they have the power to choose and to change

Homework

- Continue meal planning and contacting their buddy.

Session 7

Time split

- Review   25 minutes
- Meal Planning   25 minutes
- More on managing feelings   20 minutes
- Mothers   40 minutes
- Ending   10 minutes

Aims and objectives

- Review buddying and food in the family exercise.
- Revisit meal planning.
- Continue work on managing feelings.
- Begin work on mothers.

Review

Begin with what they have thought about the exercise about food in the family and whether they have talked to their buddy about it. You may need to spend quite a bit of time on this subject because the exercise very often produces very strong responses from the group members. It is particularly important to pay attention to anyone who has felt overwhelmed by her feelings. You don't want the power of the experience to discourage her from continuing with the group. One of the strategies you can use is to normalise her reactions, e.g. by saying "it's not surprising you feel the way you do considering how it was for you".

> Barbara had become very upset during the exercise the previous week and had sat very still while the tears rolled down her cheeks. "I can't talk about it," she said, "It's too horrible. My Mum and Dad used to shout at each other. I was terrified." At this point the group leader had used the grounding exercise to bring her back to the present and had also encouraged her to put the feelings that seemed too much into her container.
>
> The following week she did not come to the group and there was no message. After the group had been talking about their reactions for a while, somebody said, "I wonder how Barbara is. She got very upset, didn't she?" Other group members nodded and somebody else said, "I think it was too much for her".

The group leader recognised that there was implicit criticism in that comment and said, "It was very difficult wasn't it? I suppose it shows just how much feeling is locked into memories of food in our families. I can't protect you from those feelings but perhaps we can, together, think about them and the effect they have on us now. You need to use the exercises to manage feelings to help you in situations like that. We can also learn how to take care of each other. What do you think would be a good way of reaching out to Barbara now?"

What had been said about buddying had obviously had some effect because two group members said they had texted her the day after the group the previous week. She had sent them a text that just said, "Thanks!" When the rest of the group heard this they seemed to relax a little until the group leader said, "Yes, but she isn't here, is she? I will contact her after today as I always do when somebody misses a session, but what would you like to do?"

Some discussion followed and it was agreed that those who felt closest to Barbara would attempt to contact her.

Before moving on, the group leader used the opportunity to say that perhaps this was the sort of thing that might trigger a binge in Barbara, or any one of them, but that talking to someone else might mean that there was no need for a binge.

Ask them if they have thought about whether the patterns of food use in their family of origin are repeated in their current families, e.g. is food used as a comforter now, as it was then; are mealtimes structured and used in the same way?

Find out how they're doing and whether buddying is perceived as being helpful. Revisit ambivalence if necessary. Get them to think about whether they have ever had a friend with whom they could be really open. If so what was that like?

Link eating behaviour with awareness of feelings. Is it making a difference? (It should be by now.) You may need to go back to willingness to change.

Meal planning

Spend a bit of time on this. Maybe get them into small groups to discuss progress. See how they've used the sheets and give some more out. Try to field all the resistance: it takes too long, they can't plan ahead, they don't eat that much in a day (!) etc. Stress the physiological value to your body of regular feeding.

More on managing feelings

Here is another exercise that you can teach the group to help them when they are in danger of being overwhelmed. Ask them to visualise the face of someone that they know loves them and would look after them if they were in danger. Be prepared for the possibility that their immediate reaction is that there is no such person and, if necessary, get them to imagine a person with those qualities and what they might look like. Suggest that in difficult situations they could bring that face to mind. Get them to notice how they feel in their bodies when they imagine the safe face. You may want to use this exercise over the next few weeks when you will be working on mothers.

Mothers

In this exercise you are trying to get the group members to think about the qualities of mothering. What is a good mother? Everyone has an opinion on this. Get them to begin by making their own list and then maybe get them to do a whole group exercise with the flip chart. It might be a moment to see if one of them can take charge of writing up the things that people say. Try to get a good vigorous discussion going and get them to challenge and really explore different ideas. If you get into the realms of discipline, etc., there should be no problem in getting everyone involved. Try to arrive at a list of qualities of the good mother that more or less everyone can agree on.

If you have time and if it seems appropriate, get them to think about how this list compares with what their own mother was like and how they are as mothers, either to their children, if they have any, or to themselves.

> - Good mothers need to be loving, kind and understanding. Mine wasn't. I think I ate chocolate when I felt sad about that.
> - I don't know my mother. She was so unkind when I was crying and sad. Now I'm 48 she grumbles at me and says I don't care about her. I eat and eat and eat now because I don't know how to tell her she hurt me.

The underlying principle of work on mothers is that mothers are the nurturers, and most often the ones in charge of feeding. This part of the work may well lead on from the exercise on food in the family. The psychological limitations of mothers will impact on children often via the way they are fed, but also via the way they are nurtured psychologically. This is potent material for investigating eating behaviour. In the next three sessions you will be investigating how your group members have been mothered. This can be difficult material, but you have begun to identify feelings and established a buddy system as well as teaching them a good number of strategies for affect management, so there is a reasonable chance of containment.

Homework

- To continue with meal planning and contacting buddies.
- To think about what kind of mothers they are to themselves and maybe to their children.
- Be aware that some of them may not have children for a variety of reasons.

Session 8

Time split

- Review   30 minutes
- Mothers   I hour and 15 minutes
- Ending   15 minutes

Aims and objectives

- Review meal planning and buddying.
- Continue with mothers.

Review

You want meal planning to continue until Session 12 (but it may continue throughout the group), so review what is going on and how successfully they are managing to regularise eating – fewer binges, less grazing, perhaps even more proper food. Does their eating seem less frantic, less out of control? Address any ambivalence or resistance.

You want the buddying system to continue throughout the group and to stand for the possibility of a better way of managing difficulties. It may cause ripples in the group which you need to attend to. Observe whether buddying has made a difference to relationships generally. You asked them to think about their own mothering, perhaps of children, but more importantly, of themselves. Tell them you will return to this later in the session.

Mothers

If you feel this material is too much for your group just at the moment don't be afraid to defer at least a part of it. Our group leaders felt that the exercise, painting themselves and their mother, was too powerful for some groups at this point. They deferred it to later.

N.B: Don't forget the possibility that group members were brought up by someone other than their mother. A surprising number of people have been brought up by their grandmother, for example. You might want to use the word caregiver instead, although it's much less powerful.

Begin by getting them to think on their own about their mother/principal caregiver and maybe note down a few things about her (or exceptionally him) to get them into the mood. How tall was she, how was she dressed, how old was she when you were born, etc. Then as a way of providing a kind of instant picture of her, ask the group members what a typical thing that their mother would say to them would be when they were growing up. Just be aware of the possibility that this might be something quite shocking. The point is to get a snapshot of the relationship. You might want to put these phrases on a flip chart.

Then ask participants to create an image of themselves and their mother. You can choose what materials you want to provide to enable them to do this. We like paint, but it's messy and takes a long time to set up and clear away. Remember you will need to provide paper. Flip chart paper is good. Give them a whole sheet and then notice how much of it they use. If you want to, you can provide other materials for collage building as well. We are often surprised by the degree of talent shown. Some people will find it very threatening, so be sure to point out that this is not about artistic ability but about using art materials to create an image that can be shared and discussed.

When participants return to the large group circle ask them to put their images in front of them but turned away from them so that the rest of the group can see them. If there is a large number in the group the paintings can be put back to back in a row in the central open space and participants can be invited to walk round them so there is a shared viewing of them. You now want to get each painting discussed. Begin by saying that you will not be able to talk about all the paintings in this session, but that you will continue next session. The easiest way to begin may be just to ask people to talk about their painting. Be sure to acknowledge and respond in a feeling way, e.g. to someone who says she never had much of a relationship with her mother, say 'Yes, you look very isolated in your picture; you are quite a long way from your mother and not holding her hand; she is not looking at you either.' Then ask noticing kinds of questions, such as 'I see that the little girl figure in your painting has a blue dress and so does the mother'. You will find that other members of the group will take it up. This has to be repeated as each participant begins to talk about her painting.

You will need to continue with this discussion next time, since you won't be able to get through all the paintings in one session. **Be sure to keep all the paintings**. But before you finish, make a link between the relationship between them and their mothers and between them and their internal mothers. What we all need is an internally supportive mother. What are their internal mothers like and what does that have to do with their food use? Ask participants if you can keep the paintings while the group lasts.

Lauren painted a picture of a vibrant mother, centre stage in a beautiful garden, dressed in brightly coloured clothes with bright purple hair, the focus of all attention. Lauren painted herself as a poor pale little thing of no account. It took some time before she could begin to think that perhaps 'everything in the garden wasn't lovely'. She had never had that thought before. It helped her to start to make sense of how she was.

Brenda painted a picture of a mother distant from herself. She said 'my mother was stone deaf. I could never feel close to her. I think this has affected my relationships with others so I eat to feel close to something.'

Ann painted a picture of a mother walking along and herself running along behind. She said, "I always felt that if I didn't take care my mother would just leave me behind. She didn't look after me when she crossed the road. It was my job to keep close to her and, if I didn't, she wouldn't wait for me or even look round to see where I was."

Ending

The subject of mothers and mothering often upsets people. Use whatever strategies you think appropriate to manage the feelings aroused. Take time in the ending to de-role, calm and empower them.

Homework

- Meal planning again; buddying and continuing to think about mothering.

Session 9

Time split

- Review   30 minutes
- Beliefs about food   30 minutes
- Mothers continued   50 minutes
- Ending   10 minutes

Aims and objectives

- Review meal planning, buddying and mothers.
- Explore beliefs about food.
- Extend work on qualities of mothering.

Review

Spend some time checking out how things are going with meal planning and buddying. I would expect that meal planning is now beginning to have an effect on bingeing. Support and encourage them to continue with buddying. Try and identify whether particular individuals or buddy groups are having difficulties and see if the group can sort out these difficulties for them (rather than you doing it all).

Beliefs about food

Cognitive behavioural therapy works on the premise that if we know what we believe/think, we can evaluate whether it makes sense, and thus have the power to change belief systems which are irrational. I would like you to start applying this theory to the participants' beliefs about food. It is likely that many of them believe, for example, that they feel better when they eat, or that they can't manage without bingeing, or that they can't stop eating once they start. You might want to give an example. Make it up if necessary, e.g. "I used to believe that unless I ate a lot at any one time I would feel very hungry before I could eat again and that being hungry would make me feel panicky. What I've come to realise is that if I eat the right sort of food I don't get hungry so quickly anyway, and that even if I do, nothing all that bad will happen. It won't harm me to be hungry for a bit." Get them to work in groups and try to identify some of these beliefs.

The next step is to ask them for evidence for and against these beliefs. Generally speaking people can usually find evidence that their beliefs are contradicted by at least some of their experience, for instance that there have been periods when they have managed without bingeing or that they often don't feel better when they eat. Get them to identify one belief that they can challenge during the week ahead.

Mothering

First thing is to finish the reviewing of the paintings from last week. If by any chance you did finish, get them out again anyway. It's a good idea to get as much from this exercise as you can.

Don't forget that you gave them homework to think about mothering. Now is the moment to start to talk about how good they are at mothering themselves. Ask them to think about different areas of mothering: e.g. physical care – how much time and attention do they allow to care for their own bodies. Our experience has been that at least some of the group will be poor on physical self-care – not washing their hair often enough, etc. How much time they allow themselves to rest; how much time they allow themselves for friends and so on. Link self-nurture with eating. This exercise can take all the rest of this session.

Ending

As always, the subject of mothers stirs everyone up. As far as you can, make sure no one is leaving oppressed by guilt or bad memories. Use the strategies for affect management.

Homework

- Meal planning continuing (give out sheets as necessary).
- Buddying.
- Think about a particular belief about food and whether it is true.
- Continue to think about mothers and how they mother themselves.

Session 10

Time split

- Review   25 minutes
- Circle of support   30 minutes
- The patchwork mother   55 minutes
- Endings   10 minutes

Aims and objectives

- Review meal planning, buddying and beliefs about food.
- Identify support of different kinds available to them.
- Identify and represent symbolically the good experience they have had of mothering from whatever source.

Review

Ask participants about the paintings of mothers and how it affected them during the week and also enquire what they have thought about the way they mother themselves and whether they can think of ways they can improve their self-care. Spend a bit of time discussing how exactly they use the meal planning and in what way it helps, if it does. Get them to consider whether meal planning might be a way of taking better care of themselves. Be on the look out for people who don't seem to be bothering. Address the ambivalence if necessary. Review buddying briefly. Discuss whether it was helpful to identify beliefs about eating and what difference it made, if any.

Circle of support

This is an exercise designed to enable people to identify the support that is available to them from different sources. Get them to write their own name in the middle of a sheet of paper. Then ask them to draw three circles round their name. Invite them to put the names of those that they are closest to emotionally and from whom they get the most support in the innermost circle. You would expect these people to be a mixture of family and friends; members of the group might be part of this circle as well. You might want to suggest that they apply a test to these people to see if they are really in the inner circle; for example, can they tell these people about their difficulties with food or that they are coming to the group.

- I don't know who to put in the first circle. There isn't anyone that I really feel close to.
- I should have my sister in this first circle but she fell out with me and we don't speak.
- It's very difficult to reach out and ask for support from anyone else.
- My doctor is a real support to me.
- If my Nan was still alive I'd put her in that first circle.
- I can't think of anyone to put in these circles. Isn't that dreadful.
- I'm going to put the group in the first circle. People here know more about me than anyone else.

Then work out to the next circle of support, which might be wider family and friends, or might be helpful professionals such as GP or health visitor. Then a further circle which might be neighbours, child-minders, etc. The people in the various circles will vary quite a bit from person to person. The idea is to show that there is support available to them and that it consists of quite a lot of people who can help in different ways. If you think it's appropriate you could get them to put the sort of support they might get from different people. You want them to be able to think of themselves as part of a web of sustaining relationships.

The patchwork mother

The exercise you have just done is designed to represent the resources that group members perceive are available to them on the outside. This next exercise is designed to do the same thing to demonstrate the range of their inner resources.

Get them to make a list of the people in their lives, past as well as present, who have shown them the qualities that they identified as those of the good mother. You might want to get out the flip chart list of qualities that were agreed in Session 7. Then talk about how many women don't have great experience of being mothered and have to pull together the good experience from other sources to help them to mother themselves and others. Ask them to draw/paint a patchwork in which they represent each of the people they have identified. When they've finished – give them about 20 minutes or so – do what you did with the mother and child paintings: create a gallery and let everyone look at them. Then give each person a chance to talk about her work and the people who have been important to her.

Ask the group members whether there is a connection between the people in their innermost circles and the safe face or the safe place. Suggest that they think about these people during the week and consider whether they are using them to look after themselves.

Ending

Make a careful ending, remembering that most of them now have to go off and be a mother to someone else and that mothering themselves, other than with food, is a difficult business.

Homework

- To continue with meal planning and buddying and think about the exercises you have done today.
- To keep thinking about how they look after themselves.

Session 11

Time split

- Review   30 minutes
- Who can you trust?   25 minutes
- Trusting each other   50 minutes
- Ending   15 minutes

Aims and objectives

- To review meal planning, buddying and last week's exercises about the circle of support and the patchwork mother.
- To explore the issue of trusting people and compare it with trusting food.

Review

This week in the review spend a bit more time on reviewing buddying. We are working up to the end of the first 12 sessions. The overall objectives for this period are for the participants to recognise that their food use is at least in part driven by emotions and to start to think about their experience of people and how they can use them more and instead of food. Buddying is an important element in this process. Take the time to see if they are really trying to use their buddies and if not, why not. Be on the alert for the person who is willing to be phoned but never phones.

Who you can trust

The following two exercises on trust are, again, exercises that can arouse overwhelming feelings. Before you begin you may want to talk about the affect management strategies and ask them which find most useful. You can then remind them that they can have their preferred strategy ready to use if they consider that the feelings are too much for them. If you think it's useful, begin by getting participants to think back to their lives up to the age of about 18 and to think about who they could trust. Often our group members will have had their trust betrayed in quite significant ways in the past. Recognise that if your trust has been betrayed when you are young, you are highly likely to set up a system of relying on your self and food (or other substances) and that in fact this strategy may have enabled you to survive.

Even if you don't do this bit of the exercise, get them next to consider who they can trust now. What does trust mean? How do you know if someone can be trusted? Are there different levels of trust? Who can you trust with your day-to-day ups and downs (because this is what we are trying to develop)? What does it feel like not to be able to trust someone?

The problem about being betrayed is not that you don't trust anybody but that you don't know who to trust and therefore trust is placed inappropriately. Questions that can arise are:

- How do you know when to trust somebody?
- What does it mean?

The notion of testing people to see if they are trustworthy often doesn't occur to people and they may, for example, bounce from one relationship into another without any kind of testing.

Get a discussion going and try to get people to give personal examples of their experience.

Trust exercise

This exercise is old, tried and tested, but still is useful. Get participants to work in pairs. One of the pair has her eyes covered with a scarf and is then turned around several times to disorient her. The other person then leads her round the room. (Be aware that even this degree of trust is impossible for some people. We have had group participants who could not bear to have their eyes covered with a scarf; we allowed them just to close their eyes.) After a fairly short time (5 minutes or so) change places. Then get the whole group to discuss the exercise. Get them to think about the difference between their rational thinking that they are perfectly safe and whatever other feelings they have. Talk about control and being controlled and how that resonates for them.

- I don't trust myself to lead anybody else.
- I'm a perfectly competent business woman. I'm confident and self-possessed but you know, when I put that blindfold on, I changed into someone anxious, terrified and insecure.
- I couldn't bear having that scarf over my eyes. I had to get it off.
- I need to be in control. I thought that I could trust my partner to lead me but I couldn't bear not to know what was going on.
- My goodness that was powerful. It was all right to start with but then I started to have a panic attack.

The idea is to make clear that trusting people is problematic (for most people) and that it makes sense that some people (such as our participants) would deal with the anxiety by using something else (such as food).

Ending

This should make them fairly thoughtful. Make sure they leave feeling soothed and encouraged to continue the work.

Homework

- Meal planning, buddying and thinking about trust.

Session 12

Time split

- Review of last session   20 minutes
- Review of first term   50 minutes
- Self efficacy   30 minutes
- Ending   20 minutes

Aims and objectives

- To review last session, especially trust exercises.
- To review the whole of the term's work with special emphasis on what they have learned and how they have changed.
- To use Bandura's ideas on self-efficacy to strengthen their sense of self and capacity.
- To prepare them for the coming break.

Review

You may be about to have a break, so the review needs to bear that in mind. Ask them how they reacted to last week's exercises on trust and the patchwork mother. Try to consider whether they are starting to use people in a different way. Enquire about buddying and encourage them to continue with it over the break. Ask about meal planning and similarly encourage them. From the first session of next term they will be starting to work with food choice, so encourage them to continue with the meal planning over the break, especially since there will be less support available to them.

Review of first term

Here is a table of what you have done during the first term (Appendix 8).

Session	Action
1	Hopes and fears Listening Sharing information

(Continued)

2	Weightline / Lifeline Food monitoring Motivational enhancement
3	Strategies for managing overeating Names for feelings Managing feelings
4	Food monitoring Reviewing motivation Feelings in the family Managing feelings
5	Buddying Meal planning Managing feelings
6	Buddying Managing feelings Use of food in your family of origin
7	Meal planning Managing feelings Mothers
8	Mothers
9	Beliefs about food Mothers continued
10	Circle of support Patchwork mother
11	Who you can trust Trusting each other
12	Review of sessions to date

You will remember that the idea has been to be working in a cognitive behavioural way on eating behaviour, while at the same time trying to address some of the issues that seem to underlie overeating. In our view these are to do with nurturing or the lack of it and a use of food instead of people for emotional management of one's life. For that reason we have been trying to help participants to connect their eating behaviour with their feelings; educate them about feelings; get them to think about mothers and work on issues of trust of other people by buddying as well as trust exercises.

For most people this will be new territory. Use this review session to talk about how they have reacted, what has been important, what has been useful, etc. You might want to provide them with a chart of what you have done as a way of jogging their memories. You could use small groups to start this discussion but try to also talk in the whole group so that you hear at least some of their reactions.

Self-efficacy

This is an idea which potentially has great power for our participants (see http://www.des.emory.edu/mfp/BanEncy.html for a brief outline of Albert Bandura's theory). Fundamentally Bandura believes that success breeds success. Experience of being successful is a powerful means to further success. See if you can use the review session to get participants to identify their successes as a means of encouraging them, especially for the break that is coming.

Ending

The most important thing here is to encourage them for the break and do your best to ensure that they return after it. Spend a bit of time brainstorming how they are going to manage and how what they have learned will help them. Remind them about buddying, meal planning and managing feelings. Congratulate them on progress so far. Remind them that the way they deal with food has been very deep seated and will take time to change. Congratulate them on their courage in addressing these issues.

Homework

- To put into practice what they have learned.

Session 13

Time split

- Review   40 minutes
- Making a menu   25 minutes
- Food choice in your family of origin   45 minutes
- Ending   10 minutes

Aims and objectives

- To review how they feel about returning to the group and how they managed over the break.
- To do a meal planning/food choice exercise.
- To investigate food choice in their family of origin and now.
- To start the process of improving food choice.

Review

Session 12 was spent reviewing the whole of the work of the last term so there should not be any need to go over that work again, however your participants may have had a break during which they were asked to continue the work of meal planning and buddying. This needs to be followed up in the usual way. They will also have feelings about returning to the group which need to be explored. This is also a moment when group members may have dropped out. At this stage in the group their absence will really be noticed and will be unsettling for those who remain. All sorts of questions will be provoked by their absence. It is the group leader's job to manage this situation and to contain the feelings aroused. This will be particularly difficult if people have left without saying goodbye or in an angry way. It is particularly important to identify ambivalence at this point (reluctant returnees) since there may be people who have not yet started to lose weight and who are discouraged or feel that the group is not helping. You might want to return to the hopes and fears exercise from Session 1. You could use the posters that they made then and talk about them in terms of where they are now. Or you could do the exercise again, or you could do it more informally as a brainstorming on the flip chart exercise. You may also want to point out that they have tried rapid weight loss before and that it hasn't worked and that it has taken them years to get to their present weight and will take some time to alter. If it seems appropriate, you can also go back to talking about how the group tries to alter their relationship with food to make a change that will be permanent and will not depend on will power. When you feel that group solidarity and energy have been re-established, move on to the next part, but don't continue until you feel that everyone is together and the group has reformed.

By this stage in the group's development the group members are likely to have disclosed a good deal of personal information to each other. This is certain to include details of difficult situations in which they find themselves. The group has encouraged them to use each other for emotional support; that is precisely what will be beginning to happen. Review sessions will produce accounts of ongoing difficulties and exercises will provoke further disclosure of problems. Although this is an extremely important aspect of the group's development, it should not be allowed to deflect the group as a whole from its purpose of modifying food use. The group leader needs to be able to make the link between difficult experiences and inappropriate eating behaviour. Remember this is not an unstructured group but a semi-structured group. On the other hand, the discussion of emotional issues with trusted adults is exactly the strategy that we are intending to develop as a replacement for overeating. The group leader must carve a path between rigidly following the programme and abandoning it entirely in favour of open-ended interaction.

Making a menu

This is supposed to be a fairly light-hearted exercise, which ideally makes the group laugh. Ask them to write down a day's meal plans using what they know about healthy ways of eating. Stress that they should only include on this menu food that they like. (There's no point creating a menu of food that you dislike.) Get them to brainstorm what it is about the menu that makes it healthy – lots of fruit and vegetables, not too much fat, etc. Then ask them to write down what they ate yesterday. The contrast is likely to be fairly extreme. Make the point that we generally know pretty well what is good for us, but tend to be eating in a way that is not good for us.

Then talk about gradual sustainable change. Radical change (of any kind) almost never works, because it can't be sustained. You could ask for examples of this truth and/or provide your own example (make it up if necessary, e.g. "I decided I was going to walk for an hour a day – I lasted two days and then it rained so I didn't do it and I haven't walked further than the car park since"). Ask them to identify and write down one small improvement that they could make to their food choices immediately. For example, a change could be made from eating Greek Yoghurt to eating Whole Milk Yoghurt or to cutting the fat off their pork chop or to eating Lite Butter instead of full fat butter or to eating one piece of fruit a day. This is the sort of level of suggestion that will probably be necessary to help participants to understand the sort of small changes they might make. Make that their goal for the next week. Give them meal planning sheets and talk about how this change is going to be incorporated.

Remember that this sort of advice is standard diet book fare. It will only work as a strategy if the psychological mechanisms reinforcing inappropriate eating are becoming less powerful. Ask participants how they react to the idea of any modification of their eating behaviour. You may find that even minor changes are experienced as an attempt to deprive them of their essential coping mechanism.

Food choice in the family of origin and now

Many people replicate the food choices made in their family of origin because these are familiar. Generally speaking, we like what is familiar to us. However, we can also have strong emotional attachments to what is familiar. Food likes and dislikes often have emotional meaning. This exercise asks group members to think about the food in their family of origin and to reflect on how it has affected their food choices now.

Begin by getting them to write down a list of typical food that they used to eat as children. (Don't forget that they may not all have been brought up in conventional settings.) Then get them to think about that food from a nutritional point of view. Do they think it was healthy food? How has the food they provide now been influenced by the food they ate as children? What do they think about the food they provide now from a nutritional point of view? If they wanted to improve their food choices now from a health point of view, how would they do it? What are the objections to making those changes? (Here, if you want to, you can refer to current TV programmes.)

There are generally huge objections to making significant changes: family won't like it; too expensive; haven't got time, etc. Remind them that they are in the group because the way they have been eating has made them seriously overweight. How willing are they to consider making changes? Refer to the wheel of change diagram (p. 10) and get them to identify where they are on it, in relation to improved food choice.

You must also remember that if food is your comforter, favourite foods, however unhealthy, are unlikely to be abandoned without internal change.

Ending

It's very important that this material doesn't become a lecture or a telling off. It should be done in the spirit of an investigation. It is not meant to make people feel guilty, but rather interested and engaged and hopeful. Try to create and sustain this spirit as an ending.

Homework

- To make their one small change and report on it to their buddy.
- To continue with meal planning, but this time with an eye to food choice.
- To be thinking about the emotional meaning of the food choices they make.

Session 14

Time split

- Review   20 minutes
- Problem solving in relation to food choice   40 minutes
- Favourite foods and their emotional meaning   50 minutes
- Endings   10 minutes

Aims and objectives

- To review how they have managed in relation to food choice and whether they have used each other.
- To use the resources of the group to find solution to difficulties in modifying food choice.
- To think about favourite foods and the emotional meaning of them.

Review

This is crunch time. We have had a very long run up to this point and now we are looking for substantial change. When you do the review of how they have managed in making one change in their food choices, you need to be very clear about how important this is and similarly with the use of their buddy to support the change. Ask them to tell you how they incorporated the change into their meal planning sheets. Then talk about how this is the beginning of real change. Nobody is talking about deprivation – there are no depriving limits to how much they eat, but they need to take responsibility for their choice of what they eat. By now all of them should have a good idea of the emotional roots of their overeating. They should not be allowed to continue with it unchallenged.

Problem solving

There are likely to be lots of problems in instituting change. Use this time to find out what these problems are and do a whole group exercise on problem solving. Remember that your group members may well not have had any training in problem solving and may well feel that their resources for doing so are minimal. Use this as the opportunity to show them how, but also use the group as the resource.

Problem

I really like chocolate. I can't bear not to eat it.
My husband brings home doughnuts on a Sunday morning when he gets the
    papers. I can't not eat them.
I feel stupid having salad when all my friends are having chips.
My husband won't eat healthy food.
My kids hate healthy food.
I can't afford healthy food.
Etc.

Bear in mind that the practical solutions to these sorts of problems may seem obvious. What is not obvious and needs to be explored is how the dilemmas described are evidence of unresolved emotional issues; for example, the woman who can't eat differently from her friends clearly has problems with self-esteem.

The emotional meanings of food choice

This exercise is designed to help the group to identify the meanings and associations to food that is particularly liked or disliked. Get them to identify food they really like or dislike and then to associate to memories, feelings, etc., around it. The idea is to show, in yet another form, that the way we eat and the food choices we make are bound up with our emotional history.

   Be prepared for harrowing stories of being made to eat food, and violent and coercive scenes around this theme. But also address likes. Get them to think about how they use particular foods to soothe, comfort, reward, etc. Why those particular foods? Is there a history of them being used as a substitute for love? Food is often used to comfort children and to show love. Talk about how it's not necessary to eat any one particular food (or not eat it) but that if we want to eat healthily we can construct a good diet around all our likes and dislikes. Try to empower them to make good choices.

Ending

Depending on how powerful the memories are in the last exercise, you may have to soothe people and get them ready to go. Revisit strategies for management of affect. Try to let them leave feeling that they have come a long way; that they understand themselves much better; and that they can take responsibility for their choices and the way they eat.

Homework

- To make a further improvement in their food choices and to incorporate that into the meal planning.
- To think more about the emotional meaning of their food choices.
- To use their buddy to support them in doing this.

Session 15

Time split

- Review   30 minutes
- Goals for food choice   30 minutes
- Shopping   50 minutes
- Ending   10 minutes

Aims and objectives

- To review the last session especially the issue of food choice.
- To set some goals for food choices.
- To explore food shopping from an emotional and cognitive point of view.

Review

Group members have now been asked to make changes in their food choices for two successive weeks. It is very important that these changes are experienced as positive examples of how they can take responsibility for what they put in their mouths and make choices which are creative and healthy. If the changes are seen as imposed from the outside and depriving them of what they really want and like, then they will not be sustained. Try to work with them in that spirit; for example, you could ask people to tell the group what changes they have made and list them on the flip chart so that others can take down in their notebooks changes that they think they also might like to make. Give plenty of room for discussion of how making these changes has felt. Be especially alive for comments that reveal ambivalence ("Well, I suppose I have to"; "You said we had to"; "I like what I usually eat").

You can also explore how or whether the changes have been incorporated into meal planning and where they are with that. Are they continuing, is it still helpful, do they need more planning sheets, etc.? Try to underline the idea of choice. (We know that choice is constrained by all sorts of emotional and cognitive factors, but the concept of choice is liberating, just by itself.)

Goals for food choice

This may be a good moment to make sure that everyone is up to speed on what a good diet looks like. In this exercise it is particularly important that you draw on the group's own knowledge, so that you minimise the risk that healthy eating is your idea and nothing to do with them. It is impossible to guess how much people will know, so be on the look out for the people who appear to know very little.

The way we have done this sort of exercise is that we begin with the five food groups: protein, carbohydrate, fat, fruit and vegetables (vitamins and minerals), water. You can ask for examples and enter into as much detail as you think is desirable (e.g. saturated/ unsaturated fat). The concensus of all dietary advice currently seems to be that we should be eating a diet high in complex carbohydrate and low in fat and sugar. Then we get people to compile menus etc based on these principles. However you may feel this is too formal a way of going on. You could start with constructing a day's menu. They have already done this in Session 13, so it should feel reasonably easy to do as a group. You can put alternatives up alongside each other. Then you can discuss why the menu is in fact healthy (Why are you suggesting Shredded Wheat/Weetabix/porridge for breakfast. Why not have Sugar Smacks?) That way you derive the principles from their latent knowledge.

When you've done the exercise, get them to talk about how they feel about it. The constant danger is that eating well is seen as some sort of unpleasant obligation which they enter into reluctantly. What you want to convey is that they are doing something good for themselves, that they are taking power over what they put in their mouths. As we have already repeatedly explored, the link also needs to be made between finding better ways to look after themselves and liberating themselves from enslavement to food.

Shopping

This theme can be continued on the issue of shopping. Begin with how they feel about food shopping. Remember that their financial circumstances may make this a difficult task anyway. The goal is to extend the ideas of power and choice to shopping. They can use it as an opportunity to make good choices and take care of themselves (and their families) better. There may be all sorts of problems with it, however. Unfortunately food that is bad for you (loaded with fat and sugar) is often cheaper than what is good for you, e.g. biscuits as opposed to fruit. But there are choices they can make that have no financial penalty, e.g. semi-skimmed milk rather than whole milk. Wholemeal bread is more expensive than white, but not hugely so. Making food is much cheaper than buying ready meals, so that is an obvious choice. You don't have to think of the answers – get the group to problem solve.

Get them to write down the kind of shopping list they make at the moment for a week and then to go through it with each other and see how it can be improved.

This exercise can probably go on indefinitely, but make sure that at the end they have concrete goals for shopping for the next week which they have written down in their books. This exercise should obviously also be correlated with meal planning.

Suggest that they make particularly good use of their buddy for all this. In this way you will reinforce the idea that they can get something from other people and weaken their conviction that they can only manage by eating.

Ending

The important thing for the group to take away from this meeting is the idea of their power to choose, and their power to choose what will be good for them and for their families. Remind them of the changes they have planned for the coming week.

Homework

- To use what they have discussed in the group as the basis for making changes in their food shopping and meal planning.
- To use their buddy to help them.

Session 16

Time split

- Review   20 minutes
- Food choice   1 hour 25 minutes
- Ending   15 minutes

Aims and objectives

- To review the last session.
- To brainstorm problems in making good food choices.
- To address ambivalence in making changes.

Review

My guess is that there will be quite a lot to say about last week and the intervening time when they have been asked to make different/better food choices.

Be prepared for a torrent of reasons why they can't/won't change. Be sure to enquire how they have used their buddies to help them.

Food choice

This is the last session when food choice will be the focus of the whole meeting, so try to use it to review the whole subject. The fundamental principle behind it is that if they are going to lose weight they have to take in fewer calories. One way to do this is to restrict, which we know from all sorts of evidence and experience doesn't work in the long term. This programme seeks to identify the emotional purposes for which our participants use food and to free them from that way of managing their emotional lives. In the matter of food choice I have been suggesting that food choice is, to a significant extent, emotionally determined. It is much easier to eat fewer calories by changing food choice than by restricting. If food choice can be made less emotionally compulsive, participants can be freed to choose differently. This will have health benefits anyway.

The big danger is that talking directly about changing food choice is seen as an external imposition, rather than an internal choice. If you think about weight loss programmes on television, the participants constantly refer to their anxiety about what will happen if they don't do what they're told. And then the danger is that change will not be sustained. Use all your ingenuity to make the ideas and the solutions to the problems come from the group. Emphasise the use of the buddy system. Go back to the readiness to change wheel (p. 58) if you think it would be useful. Try to address the whole subject in the spirit of interest and exploration rather than 'should' and 'ought'.

You might want to go back to the whole issue of how emotion determines eating behaviour. Are they, for example, in the grip of emotion when they choose what to eat? How does their mood affect them when they go shopping? Are they maintaining eating patterns that relate to other periods of their lives? Partners and children may cause real problems. Support them to engage with their families in discussing what they eat as a family and how they can make good choices. Children will generally come along if they can be involved in the project. As with our participants, families will react better if they don't feel coerced.

Try to ensure that the discussion results in concrete intentions. If the meal planning system continues to be used it will help with making food choices at the next level, of shopping. You might want to make a group resource, e.g. a shopping guide or a collection of recipes.

Before you finish this session, review what they have learned and what they have changed in the past four sessions. You should find a greatly enhanced awareness of what they choose and why, which we would expect to be translating into action.

Ending

This is a tricky moment because of the difficulty of changing. Try to strengthen and support them before they go, and congratulate them on having the courage to change. Remind them that choice is empowering and that they have the power to choose well for themselves.

Homework

- To use all the resources available to them, including buddying to put what they have learned about food choice into action.
- To use the meal planner to help to structure food choices.

Session 17

Time split

- Review   20 minutes
- Food choice   25 minutes
- Body image and body esteem   60 minutes
- Ending   15 minutes

Aims and objectives

- To review and consolidate the work on food choice.
- To introduce the subject of body esteem.

Review

The last four sessions were spent almost exclusively on food choice. Its emotional mean-ing and its practical implications were discussed at length. At this point you should expect to see some real changes. Use the review to check out what the past week was like and what resources they used to help them to initiate and maintain change. Did they use the buddying? Have they used the meal planner? As ever, if you feel that they are ambiva-lent about change, go back to the wheel of change and/or their goals and expectations at the beginning. You have to tread the narrow path between encouragement and expecta-tion. It is, in the long run, no good if the group is depending on you to motivate them and keep them in line. On the other hand, change is difficult and support and encouragement help a lot.

Food choice

Use this time as the opportunity to trouble shoot and revisit what they have already done. All the work done in the first term should mean that they are no longer bingeing; that they recognise the need to provide food for themselves at regular intervals; that they plan what they will eat and when; that they understand at least some of the emotional power that food has for them; that they begin to be able to use people rather than food for their emotional needs; and that they start to be clearer about the changes in food choice that will help them to feel better and lose weight.

Try to identify what, in all this, needs revisiting. You may want to use more time to work on these issues that have already been covered. In any case see if you can get them to dis-cuss in concrete terms how they plan to improve their food choices for the coming week.

Body image and body esteem

Begin by getting the group to talk about how they feel about their bodies. This can turn into an orgy of self-hatred, so don't let it last too long and make sure that your response is one of sadness and concern that women can be filled with such negative and destructive attitudes to their own bodies. You may need to make the point that we are not separate from our bodies – that there is no 'my body' and 'me' as two things – I am my body and without my body there is no me. It is generally agreed that body esteem and body image are very important issues for obese people and that problems of this kind contribute a great deal to the unhappiness felt by many obese people. There is less of a consensus about whether improved body esteem leads to changes in eating behaviour. The next four sessions will focus on this area, beginning with an attempt to identify what messages the participants have taken from their history about their bodies. The hope is that by becoming more conscious of what others have told the participant about her body, she may feel freer to challenge those messages and change her image of herself. You may want to remind participants of the affect management strategies because the work on body image can be very upsetting for some people.

Get the group to settle down and become reflective and then ask them to consider the following questions. They can write down the answers if they want to, or just think about each situation as you describe it.

- What messages did you get about your body from those around you when you were:
  - an infant?
  - a pre-schooler?
  - the age of 5–11 (family, school, peer group)?
  - the age of 12–18 (thinking especially of pubertal changes and the development of sexuality)?
  - an adult?

You can expand each question by giving examples of the sorts of situations that might be relevant; for example, by asking what kind of a baby did their parents want (lively, quiet, passive, etc.)? Did they want a girl? How did the parents react to the baby learning to sit-up, crawl, walk, etc.? Clearly we are not looking for factual information so much as how the members imagine their parents received them into the world based on later experiences of their attitudes.

You can ask people to talk about these things in pairs or small groups or as a whole group – whichever seems most likely to enable the most exploration and disclosure. Be ready to hear some unpleasant stories. Remind participants that the point of this exercise is not just to drag up bad memories but to help them to understand why they might not feel good about their bodies now.

Ending

The ending needs careful handling because what we don't want is for the participants to go away having their negative body image reinforced. We are trying to identify the messages from the past, with the hope that it will give space and freedom for the group members to re-create their image.

Homework

- To continue to work on food choices using the help of meal planning and their buddy.
- To think about the effect that the messages from others about their bodies have had on their self-esteem and whether they have to agree with those messages.

Session 18

Time split

- Review   30 minutes
- Fat and thin exercise   25 minutes
- What do you value in others?   25 minutes
- What do you value in yourself?   20 minutes
- Ending   20 minutes

Aims and objectives

- To review last week's work on body esteem.
- To explore the meanings of fat and thin.
- To explore alternative ways of valuing people that are not based on size.

Review

The hope of the exercise last week is that the group will be able to recognise that they have been labelled and pathologised by their environment and that they have accepted those labels, probably because they had no choice at that point. They may also see that they have agreed to be labelled and have joined in calling themselves abusive names and learning to hate their bodies. What you are looking for is some kind of resistance to the labels and some recognition that that they can construct their own image. Look for the anger, resentment, outrage that reveals some resistance to the labels and some energy to re-make their image.

Don't forget to review briefly what has been going on about food choice.

Fat and thin

Use a brainstorming exercise to explore the meanings attached to fat and thin. Start with writing fat on a flip chart and ask the group to associate to it. There will be lots of abusive words in there, but there will also be positive words – maybe strong, powerful, cuddly, generous. Don't make any comment but go on to do the same thing on another sheet of paper for the word thin. Again there will be a lot of positive words, but some negative – maybe scrawny, weak, mean. When you have complete lists underline or ring round the positive words for fat and the negative words for thin and ask the group what they think about those words. What you are hoping is that these words which contradict the culturally approved values for fat and thin start to erode the rigid definitions of fat as bad and thin as good.

Depending on how much discussion this generates, move on to the next exercise, which makes essentially the same point.

What do you value in others?

This exercise again challenges the value system involved in using body size as a basis for esteem and self-esteem.

Ask the group to think about someone who is very dear to them and very important. Then ask them to make a list of the reasons why they like and love and value that person.

Give them some time to do this on their own and then make a list of the qualities described on the flip chart. You can confidently expect that thin does not appear on the list of lovable qualities. Try to get a discussion going on this issue.

What do you value in yourself?

Lead on from this exercise to ask the group to make a list of the qualities that make them lovable and likeable. This is usually an exceptionally difficult task for women who feel pretty bad about themselves, but persevere and insist that they try, using each other if necessary. If you like you can ask them to imagine what the person they love best would say about them and the qualities that make them lovable and likeable.

Endings

This session has involved challenging the value system based on size and shape and encouraging the group members to separate from that value system. This should have given them lots to think about. You might think about using a little bit of time to suggest that they are so used to thinking badly of themselves and so used to abusing themselves that to try and overturn that way of thinking will be difficult. Suggest that when they hear the voice in their heads that tells them the old story they try challenging that voice.

Homework

- To persevere with improving food choice, using meal planning and the support of their buddy.
- To practise talking positively and creatively to themselves about their bodies and about themselves. Talk about empowerment and how they can be good for themselves.

Session 19

Time split

- Review   30 minutes
- Food choice   25 minutes
- Guided fantasy   50 minutes
- Ending   15 minutes

Aims and objectives

- To continue to pursue improving food choice.
- To continue to explore the meanings of fat and thin.

Review

See if you can find out how the work of the last session has affected them during the week. You might want to ask if they have been more aware of how they talk to themselves and whether they have been able to find a more positive way to do it. How have they used their buddies for this task?

Food choice

Let's not lose sight of the continuing need for maintaining improved food choice. Make sure you check that out during the review and how/whether the group is using their meal planners and buddies to support their changes. Use the wheel of change if necessary and talk about empowerment.

Guided fantasy

This is an exercise which draws on one originally devised by Susie Orbach (1978) and is designed to get to some of the less conscious meanings of fat and thin. Get your group to settle down and close their eyes while you read the following text.

Imagine yourself going to a party:

- What image do you want to convey when you get yourself dressed?
- What do you want to convey by the clothes you wear?
- How are you feeling on the way to the party?
- What would you like to happen at the party?
- What are you afraid will happen?

- As you go in to the room you see people looking at you...what do you think they are thinking?
- There is food at the party...how do you deal with it?
- Someone comes up to you and starts to talk to you and shows that they are attracted to you...how do you respond?
- Is that how you want to respond?
- You see people that you know at the party...how do you deal with that?
- People start to dance...how do you react?
- It's getting to be time to go home...how do you feel?
- You get home and take off your party clothes...how do you feel about your body?
- How do you feel about the way you were at the party?

When you have finished, allow the group to come round and then invite them to explore their experience of the guided fantasy. You may want to give them copies of the questions (Appendix 9).

Ending

This exercise has the potential to get the group to reconsider the meaning of fat and thin to them and to get them to continue the process of deconstructing their self-image and body image. Try to encourage them to keep thinking about how they talk to themselves and how and whether they can change that.

Homework

- Keep going with food choice and using buddies for support.
- Think about the function of your fatness in day-to-day life.

Session 20

Time split

- Review   25 minutes
- If you really loved your body   45 minutes
- Thinking about food choice as evidence of empowerment and self-care   40 minutes
- Ending   10 minutes

Aims and objectives

- To mobilise the group members' imagination as to how better body esteem would change their behaviour.
- To ask how better body esteem would change food choices.

Review

Revisit the guided fantasy about fat and thin and see what the group members have thought about it in the intervening week. You might want to raise the issue of how the functions of fatness could be met by other means. Can participants learn to manage their feelings by other ways than by making themselves fat?

If you really loved your body

If you really loved your body, what difference would it make to your behaviour? Ask your group members to answer this question of themselves. You might want to write down on the flip chart what it would mean for them. How would it affect the way they took care of their health, their teeth, their appearance, the amount of rest they get, the food they put in their bodies, the clothes they wear? Then encourage a discussion of these issues. You could talk about what stops them doing these things, but perhaps it would be better to talk about how they can empower themselves to do them. How can they take seriously the idea that they deserve to be well-treated.

Food choice and better body esteem

If you really cherished and loved your body and believed that it deserved to be treated well, how would that affect your food choices? Get the group to consider this question for themselves and then discuss it as a whole group.

Endings

In this session you have been trying to get the group members to identify in concrete terms the effects of better body esteem. Challenge them to put these ideas into practice in the coming week. Think about how to empower them and encourage them to act on their own behalf.

Homework

- To put into practice what they have imagined and discussed in this session.

Session 21

Time split

- Review   20 minutes
- Cultural messages   30 minutes
- An acceptable me   55 minutes
- Ending   15 minutes

Aims and objectives

- To raise awareness of the cultural pressures which create body dissatisfaction.
- To create a positive image of themselves and a realistic goal for weight loss.

Review

In the last session group members were asked to consider how things would change if they really loved their bodies. Follow up on this and find out how they have been thinking and behaving as a result.

Cultural messages about size and shape

There is quite a lot of evidence to suggest that when women are confronted with images of very thin and beautiful people, their own body dissatisfaction becomes much greater and, since we are confronted with such images all the time, it is not surprising that the average woman's body dissatisfaction is normatively high.

There is interesting research about the 'Barbie' doll that suggests that Barbie is a biological impossibility (www.anred.com/stats.html). When she is scaled up to life size she becomes 6 feet tall and weighs 101 pounds. Overall, the images presented of a desirable body are completely unrealistic for most women. But, there is a danger of falling over the other side, which many feminists have done, by saying that being significantly overweight is nothing to worry about and that women should be acceptable whatever size they might be. This line will be hard for most seriously overweight women to accept, although at a deeper level self-acceptance is the first requirement for change.

In this session try to begin to explore and encourage group members' awareness of the cultural pressures on them to be a size that is quite unrealistic for most people. Get them to find examples from their own experience (TV, women's magazines, clothes shopping, etc.). The aim of this exercise is not to make them despair about their own size but to see that our culture creates a climate of thought in which most women are bound to feel dissatisfied with themselves.

An acceptable me

Use this first exercise as a lead in to talking about what they would find acceptable for themselves. Most women start a weight loss programme with wildly unrealistic ideas about what might be possible for them. The consensus is that a 5–10% weight loss will create significant health benefits and that even keeping your weight stable (i.e. not gaining more) counts as a benefit, since most overweight people steadily increase their weight until about the age of 65. However, these results have been obtained as a result of restriction and deprivation. It may well be that our participants do and will steadily lose more weight not by deprivation, but by changing their relationship with food. Get the group to talk about what they feel is a reasonable goal; then get them to paint that image. The idea here is to mobilise the positive, accepting, loving feelings they have for themselves. So the title for the painting might be 'Here is an image, painted with love, that shows how I can accept myself'.

As you did before when you asked participants to paint (Session 8), get them to display their paintings for a whole group exercise and go round getting people to talk about their image. If you can't finish the exercise in this session, be sure to continue it in the next session. **Keep the paintings.**

Ending

The hope is that this session will facilitate empowerment. Try to convey the idea that if you understand that the cultural imperative to be thin is a lie and that the promises of what you will gain when you lose weight are not likely to be accurate, then you have choice and power to decide by yourself about your body. The idea is that we free the group members to honour and respect their bodies now, never mind what the culture tells us.

Homework

- Ask group members to try to notice the images presented in advertisements, on billboards, on television, etc., and to check out their reaction and how they affect them. Ask participants to cut out the images (where possible) and present them to the group next time.
- Ask them to remember the loving image of themselves and to eat to respect that person.
- Remind them about meal planning and buddying.

Session 22

Time split

- Review   45 minutes
- Weight loss   30 minutes
- Deferred living   35 minutes
- Ending   10 minutes

Aims and objectives

- To consolidate the work of the previous session on cultural pressures by getting the group to share what they have found or noticed during the week.
- To review where they are in terms of weight loss.
- To explore whether waiting for weight loss is used as a reason for deferring living.

Review

You can expect group members to have found all sorts of material to support the idea that we are daily being presented with unreasonable images of the female body and being made to feel bad for not being that way. Encourage them to think of their wish to lose weight as something they do for themselves and for their health, rather than as an attempt to meet external cultural standards. (In the first interview of a cohort of research participants, worries about health were the most important anxiety reported.) Follow up on the paintings from last time and try to get the group in touch with how nice it would be to love and honour their own bodies. Complete this exercise if you did not do so last week. In any case get the paintings out and use them to help the group to get in touch with loving feelings towards their bodies.

Weight loss and where they are with it

If the whole theory behind this group has anything going for it then it should lead to steady weight loss throughout the life of the group for most people. In fact our experience has been that participants often do not start to lose weight until the second term of the intervention but then continue to do so after the end of the intervention. We have not so far, in the programme, explicitly discussed whether they are losing weight but we are now approaching the two-thirds mark in the life of the group. If the treatment is going to work, it should be working by now. Bearing in mind the work of the previous session, get the group to discuss whether they have lost weight and what has been most useful in enabling them to do so. Conversely, get them to think about what gets in the way or slows them down and how that can be addressed. They should be familiar enough by now with the concepts involved to enable them to figure the answers out for themselves. Make sure this exercise doesn't turn into a competition, but more of an opportunity to share what has been helpful and ways they have found to help themselves. Give this exercise as much time as it needs.

Deferring living while you wait for weight loss

Most women are familiar with the idea of having a range of clothes in their wardrobes, some of which at least will be of a size they once might have been and hope to be again. Many will also recognise the reluctance to buy clothes, in the hope that when eventually they do, they will be a smaller size. These are small examples of a much more pervasive temptation to put life on hold until we are the 'right' size. Try to address this with the group. You might want to ask them whether they have plans for what they will do when they are thinner – and then ask them why they don't do those things now. You could also ask them what they would regret not having done if they were to die tomorrow, and whether they are deferring doing that thing until they get thin. When this way of going on is really problematic it prevents women going out, getting a job, starting to exercise, etc.

A variation on this theme is to blame your weight or your body shape for everything that is wrong or unsatisfying in your life and to imagine that when you eventually lose weight, everything will miraculously be wonderful. How would it be instead to think that losing weight will be good, but will not change the essential you and will almost certainly not change your relationship or your job or anything else of importance. Use the notions of body acceptance that we have been working on to encourage the group members to take a hold of their lives now. Try hard to make this exercise encouraging and supportive and not a telling off.

Ending

This may have felt a hard-hitting session to some people. Try to get them to talk in terms of opportunity and choice. Aim for empowerment..

Homework

- To put into practice all that they have learned about how they use food and to use their buddy to help them do so.

Session 23

Time split

- Review   30 minutes
- Positive talk   40 minutes
- Body appreciation   25 minutes
- Endings   25 minutes

Aims and objectives

- To consolidate the work on body esteem.
- To teach the principles of positive self-talk.
- To encourage body appreciation.

Review

The last session directly addressed weight loss. Find out what the group have been thinking about it and deal with any problems it has created. For some people it may have been discouraging or demotivating. Try to get the group to support and encourage them.

Positive (self)-talk

We have already used the idea that there might be different voices inside our heads, so the notion of self-talk should not be too difficult to grasp. What this exercise addresses is the negative messages that many women constantly give themselves about their bodies and how they reinforce those messages by using magazines, etc., to practise a sort of body fascism. If you look at women's magazines at the lower end of the market you will see that they are full of abusive comments on the bodies of celebrities. If even the bodies of celebrities are up for this kind of criticism it is no wonder that ordinary women are upset about their bodies. Refer to the exercise the group did as homework for Session 21 where they found images of very thin women. Suggest that paying attention to these sorts of images is probably very unhelpful. Try to get them to make conscious the internal commentary that these images inspire in them. Ask them about whether they make disparaging comments about their own bodies to other people (I'm so fat these days; I hate my legs, etc.) and whether they can think of alternative ways of talking (I'm doing better at looking after myself these days; I have a weight problem but I'm working on it). You might suggest that the internal dialogue of hate can be replaced by the message, 'I'm OK'. This message is not unrealistic (i.e. it doesn't try to get our participants to say to themselves 'I am beautiful' which for most will be impossible). Alternatively you could ask the group to devise their own messages to themselves in pairs, using each other to help them.

Body appreciation

It's a truism that you don't appreciate your body until it doesn't work for you any more. Ask the group about their experience of illness/injury/disability and the effect it had/has on their physical functioning. Most people can remember how problematic even minor malfunctioning of our bodies can be (e.g. a sprained ankle). Then ask them to construct a list (a poem?) of the things they are grateful for in their bodies – a kind of thank you list to their bodies. Some people will have particular reasons for gratitude as a result of comparison with others ('I am so glad that I don't have rheumatoid arthritis like my mother, which eventually destroyed her mobility and her physical strength completely'). The idea is to complement the first exercise by showing how foolish our obsession with appearance is in comparison to the real needs of our bodies. Maybe you can suggest that they add some mantra of gratitude for their bodies' functioning to the positive self-talk message that they developed in the first exercise.

Ending

This is the last session that will be primarily devoted to body image and body esteem. Ask the group where they are with it at this point.

Homework

- To practise positive self-talk and body appreciation and to report to their buddy on how they are doing.

Session 24

Time split

- Review   20 minutes
- Review of programme   1 hour 10 minutes
- Preparation for break   30 minutes

Aims and objectives

- To review the last session.
- To review the work of the whole programme to date.
- To prepare for a break.

Review

Spend a relatively short amount of time on reviewing how they have managed with positive self-talk and body appreciation. Find out if they managed to use their buddy to help.

Review of the programme so far

You will remember that Session 12 was a review of the programme to this point. Session 24 marks the two-thirds point in the programme. There are 12 weeks to go. The major task for the next 12 weeks will be to add the issue of activity to the existing themes and to carry forward the lines of thinking that have already been established (e.g. food choice, emotional use of food, etc.). This session should be used to discuss progress so far.

There are a number of ways you might do this. One would be to return to the hopes and fears list that they made at the beginning. However it may produce more focused reflection if you provide a list of areas for review, such as the following:

- Awareness of emotional eating
- Awareness of habitual patterns of food use (maybe from family of origin)
- Awareness of feelings
- Capacity to nurture self
- Capacity to eat regularly rather than chaotically
- Capacity to use people instead of food to deal with feelings and events (use of buddy as well as others)
- Capacity to eat more according to physical need and less according to emotional need
- Food choice and how it has changed
- Body image/acceptance and how it has changed
- Valuing yourself and the effect it has on your behaviour.

Don't forget about self-efficacy. You are looking to identify success, rather than bewail failure. Remind them about the wheel of change. It is progress to move from pre-contemplation to contemplation; returning to the stage before is built into the model – it is to be expected.

Here is a table of what you have done in the 24 weeks to date, just to remind you. You might want to reproduce it for the group so they see what a huge amount of work they have done (Appendix 10).

Session	Action
1	Hopes and fears Listening Sharing information
2	Weightline/lifeline Food monitoring Motivational enhancement
3	Strategies for managing overeating Names for feelings Managing feelings
4	Food monitoring Reviewing motivation Feelings in the family Managing feelings
5	Buddying Meal planning Managing feelings
6	Buddying Managing feelings Use of food in your family of origin
7	Meal planning Managing feelings Mothers
8	Mothers
9	Beliefs about food Mothers continued
10	Circle of support Patchwork mother
11	Who you can trust Trusting each other
12	Review of sessions to date

13	Making a menu
	Food choice in family of origin
14	Problem solving for food choice
	Emotional meaning of food choice
15	Goals for food choice
	Shopping for food
16	Food choice
17	Food choice
	Body image and body esteem
18	Fat and thin
	Qualities you value in others
	Qualities you value in yourself
19	Food choice
	Guided fantasy of going to the party
20	If you really loved your body
	Food choice
21	Cultural messages about shape and size
	Image of an acceptable me
22	Progress on weight loss
	Deferring living while waiting for weight loss
23	Positive self-talk
	Body appreciation
24	Review of sessions to date

Ending

You are hoping that the result of this session's work will be that they leave feeling impressed by their own progress and energised to continue. If this session is the beginning of a break, be sure to ask them how they plan to continue the work of the group during the break. Remind them about buddying and give them more meal planning charts if they want them. Try to get them to leave feeling encouraged and empowered.

Homework

- To reflect on all that they have done so far and to use that experience to help them to make the changes they need to make.

Session 25

Time split

- Review   20 minutes
- Activity audit   45 minutes
- Emotional eating revisited   45 minutes
- Ending   10 minutes

Aims and objectives

- To introduce the subject of activity and to carry out an activity audit.
- To revisit the issue of emotional eating.

Review

If you have just had a break, you need to get the group to come back together. By now that should not be a difficult task. Enquire how they managed over the break with buddying, meal planning, food choice and body esteem. When you feel the group has cohered again, introduce the fact that this is the beginning of the third and last term and allow room for reactions to that fact. You can expect a good deal of disappointment and concern. Be alive also to the possibility that it may be in part a relief to think that the group is coming to an end. You might want to review hopes and fears if it seems appropriate, and/or motivation for change in this last lap. Talk about how this last 12 weeks is devoted to the issue of activity and to reviewing everything you have done so far with the idea of ensuring that everything is clear and available for use. Lifestyle change (which is what you are about) is generally reckoned to take six months to fix in place. Your participants will now have been in the group for six months. This last three months should help them to ensure that the changes are well integrated into their lives.

Activity audit

Most people, especially most overweight people, take vanishingly small amounts of exercise. There are some statistics which show that up to 70% of the population is active for less than 30 minutes per week. It is likely that your participants are among them. We will deal in coming weeks with the history of their activity and their feelings about it, but for this week we will concentrate on getting them to try to estimate how much activity they took the previous day.

You might at this point want to discuss the term 'activity' as opposed to 'exercise'. Very few overweight people want to engage in formal exercise, but most people can at least consider increasing their physical activity. Obviously if you start from a very low base line, increasing activity is not very hard. From a weight loss point of view, exercise is surprisingly ineffective. You have to engage in really heroic amounts of it in order to create weight loss. However, exercise is much more useful for maintaining weight loss and for producing the by-products of improvement in mood and general improvements in health and well-being, such as a reduction in constipation, improved sleep patterns and reduction in stiffness. Improved mood and well-being is, in turn, likely to enable adherence to lifestyle change and maintain better self-esteem. Everything is to be said for it then.

Use this opportunity to get your participants to make a list of the activity they undertook the previous day. Get them to do it very systematically for the whole day, including things like going upstairs, walking across the car park, taking rubbish to the bin, walking round the garden, etc.

Then ask them how they think they could increase their activity by a small amount, let's say 10%. Be ready for all the reasons why not and go back to the wheel of change if necessary. Focus on how that change could be built into their day. Many authorities think that home-based and integrated activity is by far the most hopeful way of increasing activity. Get the group to brainstorm ideas and put them on the board. Try to get them to commit to trying at least one of them. Don't forget those with disabilities, but keep remembering that any increase in activity means an increase for that particular person, even if it is as simple as a disabled person doing leg or arm lifts. Anyone who is disabled is also likely to have had exercises recommended. Ask them what they are and to demonstrate them to the group.

Emotional eating revisited

Early sessions of the group were concerned with getting participants to make the link between their feelings and their eating behaviour. Ask them where they are in relation to these ideas now. Are they more aware of the links; what do they do about them? Are there still times when they are liable to eat emotionally? What are they?

What you should expect to hear is that they are very much more aware of the way they use food and very much more capable of finding other ways to handle their feelings. Let them tell the story of their successes and failures and be appropriately encouraging and proud.

Ending

There may be quite a mixture of feelings in the group at this point. They have started on the final section of the group, but the consolidation should have helped them to realise how far they have come. Give an opportunity for the voicing of these feelings

Homework

- Ask for a commitment to increasing activity in at least one way during the week.
- Suggest that they observe whether their eating behaviour is still being influenced by their feelings.
- Remind them of meal planning and buddying.

Session 26

Time split

- Review   20 minutes
- History of activity   50 minutes
- Food in your family revisited   40 minutes
- Ending   10 minutes

Aims and objectives

- To explore the history of their relationship with activity and exercise.
- To revisit the subject of food in their family of origin and enquire to what extent that still affects their food use and choices now.

Review

Your participants were asked to commit themselves to increasing their activity in some way during the week. Ask them what happened, what they did, how it felt, etc. This is an area where the buddy can easily be of use (going for a walk together; agreeing to walk to school with the children together; meeting to go somewhere together, etc.). Be especially on the look out for reports of improved well-being and equally for difficulties caused by size. ("I want to do more, but I get so hot and sweaty if I even walk to the shops that I feel a freak"). Get the group to produce the ideas and solutions.

History of group members' relationship with activity and exercise

Many, many people have horrid memories of being mocked or rejected for their difficulties with physical activity. Many more have bad memories of exercise as uncomfortable or even painful. Much formal exercise training in schools has been (and maybe still is, in some places) directed at the naturally slim and athletic and everyone else has been made to feel bad. You may want to revisit the management of feelings before the group does this exercise.

Ask the group members to think about these issues. You might want to prompt them by getting them to think about:

- Their families' attitude to activity. Did they come from sporty and active families? What was the role model provided by their mothers? Was there encouragement and support for activity? How was activity seen in relation to femininity?

- What was their experience in junior school? Often children quite enjoy activity at this stage and have good memories of skipping, running, etc. Junior school sports days are often rather nice occasions. However, this isn't always so and fat children, in particular, may have a miserable time.
- Problems often start, for girls, with puberty. Most girls abandon all formal exercise at around the age of 13. This means that even when they have enjoyed being on the hockey team or doing judo or dancing class, they drop out and never again engage in regular exercise. This is usually prompted by changes in body shape, increasing self-consciousness and peer pressure. Explore all this with the group.
- In late adolescence and young adulthood a lot of girls get at least some exercise from dancing, but it is highly likely that your group members will have been overweight by this stage and more likely to be sitting holding their mates' handbags than being on the dance floor themselves. Explore these issues.
- Children make most women more active, but serious overweight will make this difficult. Find out what has happened to them in relation to activity since their early twenties. Expect to hear a story of steadily declining fitness.

The point of this exploration is not just to hear the story, but to think about how the history has affected their attitudes to exercise and activity now. For many women these are poisoned areas. Go back to the idea of activity as opposed to exercise and get them to revisit both its benefits and how increased activity could be built into their day.

Food in the family revisited

Get the group to think about the work you did in relation to the social and emotional experience of food and meals in their family of origin. Talk about what they have come to realise about how that experience affected what they did with food in adult life. Talk also about food choice in their family of origin and the meanings of their favourite and least favourite foods. Where are they in relation to all of this now? Do they feel that they can leave those memories and habits behind? Can they make choices about how mealtimes are conducted, that result from choice in the present?

There may be a temptation to give easy quick answers to these questions. Given that we are trying to change the relationship our clients have with food, try to stick with it long enough to uncover the difficulties. It may be helpful to think about a process of growing out of bad old habits, even/especially where those had good associations, into some more adult relationship with food.

Ending

It is possible that revisiting this area may have made the group rather upset. If so, soothe and calm them before they go. Talking about their power in the present, reminding them of their adult status, focusing on growth and change, may all help.

Remind them that they are engaged in a process of lifestyle change and that food choice and increased activity are basic elements of it.

Homework

- Continue to work on small increases in activity, which are integrated into their day.
- Continue with food choice, meal planning and buddying.

Session 27

Time split

- Review   15 minutes
- Stepometers   45 minutes
- Feelings revisited   45 minutes
- Ending   15 minutes

Aims and objectives

- To introduce the use of stepometers and practise using them.
- To revisit the subject of feelings.

Review

Ask the group members how they have managed with a further increase in activity. Again try to use the group to deal with problems and produce solutions and ideas. Listen for complaints from disabled or very obese members; pay special attention to getting them to start to find a way for themselves. Serious obesity is disabling in itself so any improvement in mobility, etc., is highly desirable. Enquire how the ongoing tasks of food choice and buddying are going.

Stepometers

There is a lot of evidence that walking is the simplest, cheapest, easiest, and most available form of exercise for many people. Because it is load bearing it strengthens the skeleton and is preventative for osteoporosis. It improves breathing, strengthens major muscle groups, increases movement range, etc. Stepometers are a convenient way both to measure existing levels of activity and to measure increases. Give each of your participants a stepometer and let them look at it. Some will probably have seen one before and some will know about them. The problem for using them with obese people is that their operation depends on the swing of a pendulum as movement is made; usually this is registered with the movement of the hip as a person moves. However the movement of the hip of a very large person may not be enough to register. The alternative is to place the stepometer on the lower leg, so that each time the leg swings it will register. This style is a problem for driving because a movement will be registered each time the foot is moved to depress the pedal but in other situations may be useful. Start by explaining how they work and getting the group to position the stepometer on their hip. Spend the next half hour or so practising placing the stepometer and checking that it registers walking. Get the group to count the steps they take and check their counting against the stepometer, repositioning it until it registers the right number of steps. This exercise will count as a work out in itself for some members, so just be aware of how they are managing.

Then discuss with the group how they can use the stepometer during the week. Be aware of the less mobile and disabled members. They can use the stepometers to register leg movement while they are sitting or arm movements if they fix them to their arms, but it may be that they are simply not useful to those members. Be careful to respond to the feelings that will be aroused by this. Ask group members to record their daily totals. Deal with issues of whether they can tell their families, etc.

Feelings revisited

Part of the basis of this whole programme was the idea that people who use food often have limited emotional vocabulary and may not be able to identify what they feel. You will remember that you did a lot of work around words for feelings, feelings in the family and how they were expressed and dealt with, feelings most familiar to the members, etc. Revisit this whole area and ask the group where they are with all of this now. What we are hoping for is the capacity to identify and name feelings before they get buried by food, so that there is at least a choice of response. Explore how far the group members have come on this journey.

Ending

The stepometers will probably have made the group feel quite excited and they may be pleased to have a new toy to play with. Encourage moderate increases in activity. Don't forget to pay attention to the reactions of those who are less mobile. Watch out for reactions to revisiting the material on feelings. For some people this may be difficult work.

Homework

- Remind them about recording totals.
- Tell them that it is easy to lose the stepometer so to be careful about how they fix it on.
- Encourage buddying and continued vigilance about food choice.

Session 28

Time split

- Review   20 minutes
- A changing vision of their physicality   20 minutes
- Trust, buddying and relationships revisited   1 hour
- Ending   20 minutes

Aims and objectives

- To explore the experience of using the stepometer.
- To think about a changing vision of their physicality.
- Trust, relationships and buddying revisited.

Review

One of the major tasks of this session is to find out how the group got on with the stepometers. I would be surprised if anyone has not tried it out, but if there is someone who hasn't, that obviously needs some exploration. As ever we are interested not just in the information, but also in the emotional experience.

There is a scale of how many steps a person should be taking to be active and healthy. The minimum desirable total is 10,000. I would be extremely surprised if any of the group is taking that many and for the moment I would not be giving them this kind of information (although some may know or find out anyway). About 70% of the population are taking less than 3,000 steps per day. (Apparently, the norm in the USA is 1,500.) The point for us of course is not how many steps the group members take, but how successful they are at increasing the total. Get each of them to identify an average figure for each day from what they have recorded and then to set themselves a target for the next week to increase that average. Small increases that can easily be met are the ideal.

A changing vision of their physicality

Spend some time on exploring the feelings round the whole experience. We are looking for empowerment and improved well-being. Ask them if they can begin to have a different vision of their physicality. What is their hope of how their physical self-image and well-being can change and develop? Support and encourage the group.

Trust, buddying and relationships

Go back to the whole idea that overeating may very well involve choosing food rather than people. You might want to revisit the whole subject of trust in people and acknowledge that many of your group may have very good reasons to feel mistrustful of people. You can talk about the advantages of food as reliable, accessible, controllable, etc., but get the group also to talk about the disadvantages of shame, physical limitation, body image problems in relation to obesity. Then talk about the group as a way of testing whether sharing with other people can be possible. Ask them to talk about how this particular aspect of the group has been for them. Develop this idea in terms of buddying. Have they allowed themselves to take advantage of the opportunity to have a buddy? Could they use that opportunity more in this last part of the programme? Go on to ask them what the group has done for their trust and relationships with people outside the group. In the past, group members have reported considerable improvements in their relationships of all kinds. Explore this whole issue with them.

Ending

In this session you have gone from the fairly straightforward subject of the use of stepometers to much more complex and emotional issues of physical self-image and relationships with people. For some people this will have been a powerful session. Soothe and calm the group and get them to acknowledge how far they have come.

Homework

- To continue to use the stepometers and record the daily totals.
- To think about their developing physicality and construct a new image of their physical selves.
- To be aware of relationships and take maximum advantage of the support available to them through buddying.

Session 29

Time split

- Review   45 minutes
- Mothers and nurturing revisited   60 minutes
- Ending   15 minutes

Aims and objectives

- To continue to explore the use of the stepometer.
- To emphasise the vital function of relationship.
- To revisit mothering and nurture.

Review

This is the second week that the group have had a stepometer; again take time to see how they are using it and whether their activity levels are increasing. Pay particular attention to whether they are able to build in activity to their day, which will increase the chance of it being maintained. Ask whether increased activity is having an effect on them, both physically and emotionally. Exercise tends to decrease appetite via the lowering of insulin levels, so you might want to make enquiries in that area. Follow up the whole area of a change in body image and an improved sense of their own physicality.

You can also ask whether they have been able to use their buddy to reinforce increased activity. This follows on from the revisiting of trust, buddying and relationships in the last session, so use the opportunity to ask them what they've been thinking about during the week. This is a fundamental issue for the programme which rests on the premise that emotional food use needs to be replaced by a person. Challenge them on it, if necessary.

Mothers and nurturing revisited

This is another crucial area for the programme. The hypothesis is that internal and external nurture are necessary for us if we are to manage our lives without too much distress. Nurture that has not been good enough in the beginning is likely to leave us with a deficit that has to be filled some other way and in the case of our participants has been filled by food. The big issue for the programme is whether participants can:

- Recognise the deficit
- Recognise the use of food to fill it
- Learn to nurture themselves
- Learn to find nurturing relationships of all kinds
- Let go of food use.

Use this session to explore where they are in this process. You could ask questions such as: To what extent is food still your best friend? How are you doing in becoming your own best friend? What else do you need to do to take care of yourself better? How are you doing at finding people to help take care of you? How are you doing at letting go of the role of taking care of everyone else but yourself? What changes can you continue to make in this direction?

Try to talk in the particular rather than the general and enquire what small change could be made in this coming week.

Enquire about the internal critic and slanderer. What is their internal commentary on themselves sounding like? This relates back to the typical comment from their mother (Session 8). You may want to revisit this, or not; it is difficult territory for a lot of women. At this point in the programme it may be better to build for the future.

Think about your own modelling of caregiving in the group and the group's modelling of caregiving to its members. Ask about this experience and what they have learned from it.

Ending

We are now into the last eight sessions of the programme. This needs to be kept in mind so that the group can be properly prepared for life after the group. Ask them to use the principle of people instead of food this week as a practice for when they will not have the group supporting them every week. Ask them how they will use their internal nurturer and other people to help them continue with the meal planning and activity programme they have devised for themselves in this coming week. Really challenge them to use what they have learned.

Homework

- To continue to use the stepometer as a way of monitoring and increasing activity.
- To focus on the use of other people rather than food to get them through the week.

Session 30

Time split

- Review   30 minutes
- Motivation revisited   70 minutes
- Ending   20 minutes

Aims and objectives

- To continue to discuss activity levels and their impact on participants' well-being.
- To revisit motivation.

Review

Last week you challenged the group to put into practice what they have learned about the use of people rather than food. Make that the focus of the review today. You can build in the continuing monitoring of activity levels by getting them to talk about how they used people to enable them to increase their activity. Use the inevitable ambivalence to revisit the motivational wheel.

Motivation revisited

We have used the motivational wheel repeatedly during the programme for a number of purposes:

- To demonstrate that ambivalence is ordinary and that we are all continually fluctuating in our commitment to fulfilling our goals.
- To deal with resistance to change.
- To place the responsibility for change in the lap of the group members and not with anyone else.
- To help people to start again in the face of lapses and failures.

Draw it or get out a diagram and use it as a way to discuss their change process over the life of the programme. They will shortly have to manage without the group. Ask them how they are going to deal with lapses in their eating behaviour or their activity levels. There has recently been more work done on the problem for maintaining weight loss of black and white thinking (Byrne et al., 2004). It is as if dieters say: "If I don't eat what I should, then I should just jack in the whole attempt to make good food choices." The research suggests that black and white thinkers are more likely to regain weight. We would expect that all the work that has been done on motivation throughout the group would have eroded a lot of these tendencies in group members, but now is a good time to check this out. The motivational wheel shows that relapse is ordinary and that the task is just to climb back on and get on with it. Have a good, full discussion around all this. Make it as particular as you can and try to relate it to food choice and activity levels.

Ending

Keeping in mind the coming end to the group, get them to use the motivational wheel this week to help them to think about how they will manage when the group has ended. Can they use it during the week to help them to survive the inevitable mistakes and imperfections in their lifestyle changes? Suggest that these issues can be discussed with buddies and others. (Partners and children might well benefit from using the wheel.)

Homework

- To continue with attention to meal planning, food choice and activity levels.
- To use the motivational wheel to support and encourage commitment to change.
- To use other people to discuss the issues that arise.

Session 31

Time split

- Review   30 minutes
- Trust revisited   75 minutes
- Ending   15 minutes

Aims and objectives

- To review the use of the motivational wheel.
- To revisit the subject of trust.

Review

Ask the participants how they were able to use the motivational wheel to help them with the core aims of the programme:

- People instead of food.
- Improved food choice.
- Increased activity.

If this sounds a bit challenging, it is meant to. We are coming close to the end. The participants have had a long run up to the point of being able to maintain the lifestyle changes that they have been taught; the moment of truth is fast approaching. You need to prepare them for managing without the group. You have given them strategies to manage feelings. You need to help them to be confident in their use of the tools you have given them to maintain change. Ask them to describe in detail how in the past week they have used food rather than people, improved food choice and increased activity. Monitor the use of the stepometers.

Trust revisited

The difficulty for those whose trust has been betrayed, especially when this has happened early in life, is not only that they may find it difficult to trust anyone thereafter, but also that they may not know whom to trust. You will remember that we explored this via trust exercises, by thinking about the qualities of a good (m)other and by exploring circles of relationship and investigating the differences in intimacy between us and the various people in our world. The task for today is to revisit this area in order to consolidate the capacity for relationship that we have been trying to foster via the group and the use of buddying. You might want to begin with asking the group about the qualities of a person they can trust. Try to make this a concrete rather than abstract exercise: e.g. think of someone you trust; what is it about that person that makes it possible to trust her? It may also be useful to talk about the impossibility of absolute trust – we want to be able to trust someone 100% but 95% is a more realistic goal. Get them to think about whether they themselves are trustworthy. Are there limits and hiccups in their trustworthiness? Can that be all right? Is it even rather realistic and human? What have they learned about trust from the experience of being in the group?

Take the opportunity for a painting exercise. Ask the participants to paint a trusting relationship in their own lives (past or present, but preferably present). Remind them that trust is in all relationships, not just the closest and most intimate. Reassure them, as usual, that this is not about their artistic skills but about using something other than words to explore feelings. Then follow the usual format of giving them time to paint, viewing the paintings and discussing them one by one. If necessary/desirable the discussion can continue in the following week.

Remember, you are trying to foster their capacity to trust other people and to be able to determine who can be trusted.

Ending

This exercise may have left some people feeling a little shaky. Remind them about strategies for affect management. Take some time to soothe and calm the group before they leave. Remind them of how far they have come. Encourage and congratulate them on their courage and perseverance. Allow them to feel proud of themselves and each other.

Homework

- In their ongoing attempts to use people instead of food, ask the group members to think about trust and how they can find people that they can trust to support and help them.
- Ask them how they can be people who can be trusted by others.
- Mention the stepometers and food choices.

Session 32

Time split

- Review   20 minutes
- Trust revisited continued   50 minutes
- Relationships revisited   40 minutes
- Ending   10 minutes

Aims and objectives

- To continue with discussing trust and the paintings generated last week, as necessary.
- To review their closest relationships.

Review

As usual we are trying to keep an eye on the continuing process of attention to food choice and meal planning together with activity and the use of the stepometer, while also reviewing how these activities have been affected by the particular emotional focus of the previous week. So the question for this week is: 'How did the work we did on trust last week affect what happened for you this week?' You are looking for steadily increasing capacity to make good choices about relationships of every kind and a better capacity to use trustworthy people for support for lifestyle change.

Trust painting exercise continued

Take whatever time you need to conclude this exercise.

Relationships revisited

If you have time you might want to do this exercise, but it echoes themes that have already been revisited, so you can use all the time for finishing the painting exercise if you want to.

One of the ideas that has been implicit in all that has been done in the group so far is the idea of emotional growth and change. The whole issue of weight loss and lifestyle change has been built around the idea that we have ways of being in the world that make perfect sense in terms of our history, but which may be time-expired in terms of our present lives. Most obviously it may have made very good sense for our participants to use food rather than people earlier in their lives; it may make much less sense now. The underlying hypothesis of the programme is that lifestyle change depends on change in the inner world.

A similar way of thinking can be applied to our participants' relationships. It may well be true that it has made perfect sense for them to be isolated or lonely or suspicious of other people. As they grow and change this will be less necessary and less desirable. Try to explore the whole area of how changes in them can change their relationships. How does their different way of being affect relationships with their children, their partner, their wider family, their work colleagues, their friends, etc.? How will believing that relationships can grow and develop help them to manage their lives better?

Ending

The hope is that all this talk of trust and relationships makes our participants feel safer and stronger about themselves and about other people. Try to get them to think about how this work can support the lifestyle changes they are pursuing.

Homework

- To continue with monitoring food choice, meal planning, increased activity and use of the stepometer and to think what relationships have to do with all that.

Session 33

Time split

- Review   40 minutes
- Food choice revisited   60 minutes
- Ending   20 minutes

Aims and objectives

- To review how relationships affect eating behaviour and activity levels.
- To revisit food choice.

Review

The homework from the previous week was to review how relationships affect everything to do with their eating behaviour and activity levels. Initiate discussion on this issue. Be alert for reports of changes – after all we are close to the end and would expect there to have been changes in this area. Maybe brainstorming how they can manage relationships/feelings without harming themselves would be useful. It may be appropriate to role play particular situations to create a better ending. This may also be the time to review how they are continuing to use the stepometers.

Food choice revisited

When this area was originally explored in the second term we suggested that food choice is probably very much influenced by the past and by emotional attachment to certain foods. Making good food choices (in the sense of healthier) was presented as an opportunity for the group members to treat themselves well and to look after themselves appropriately. Food choice was then included in the system of meal planning which should by now have become routine. Some researchers think that sugar particularly corrupts the ability to choose food appropriately; many think that we have a stone-age preference for fat and sugar. However, some researchers also think that if exposed to a nutritionally more satisfying diet for a reasonable period, we will come to prefer those foods. This may be a way to explore members' progress in this area. It is clear that food choice built on denial and deprivation is unlikely to work. The reports you hear may demonstrate that truth, but you can be encouraging the continued reframing in terms of "I am doing something good for myself", "I deserve to eat well", "I am important enough to take care of myself". Stories of persistent choice of what is clearly unhealthy might prompt you to revisit the whole business of the influence of the past. Because we are very close to the end, focus more on the power to choose, as an adult, in the present. You might want to repeat the exercise of getting members to write down what they now think of as a desirable menu for the day, bearing in mind all they have learned, and then getting them to write down what they ate yesterday. I would be surprised if the contrast was as great as when they first did this exercise four or five months previously. You might want to get them to look it up in their notebooks to check.

Ending

Only three more sessions to go! Spend a bit of time on how they will prepare themselves to manage on their own.

Homework

- Ask the members to focus on consolidating their ability to make good food choices and to think about how they will maintain that when they no longer have the group to support them.

Session 34

Time split

- Review   20 minutes
- Hopes and fears revisited   40 minutes
- Body esteem revisited   40 minutes
- Ending   20 minutes

Aims and objectives

- To review the use of the stepometers in relation to increasing activity and promoting well-being.
- To review hopes and fears from Session 1.
- To revisit body esteem.
- To discuss the possibility of a follow-up session in three months.

Review

How have the group got on with the stepometers and more importantly have they increased their activity? How useful have they been in terms of increasing activity? What increases in their activity can they identify? How has the activity affected their eating behaviour? How has it affected their sense of well-being? What resolution would they like to make about increasing activity and/or maintaining increased activity levels? How can increased activity be integrated into their everyday lives? Are there other sorts of activity that they would like to explore? How could they go about doing that?

What were their thoughts about the ending and how they would maintain good food choices? What have they thought about in relation to these issues in the intervening week?

Hopes and fears revisited

It's a long time since the group first started and they first mapped out their hopes and fears. You may have returned to these lists in the intervening time, but now is the moment for using them to review where they were then and where they are now. This is the first of three sessions which will be devoted to recognising changes that have been made, consolidating what has been done and making plans and resolutions for the future. The hopes and fears charts will probably also give you the chance to talk about the group process, since it is likely that the group itself was a source of anxiety at that first meeting. You may want to use this session at least in part, for discussing what hasn't happened, and what has been disappointing. If you allow those sorts of things to be said now, it is much less likely that the whole experience will be rubbished at a later date. It is probable that group members will be disappointed with their weight loss, since it is extremely difficult to lose large amounts of weight. Loss of 5–10% of baseline weight is regarded as success and even maintaining a stable weight (i.e. not gaining any more) is increasingly seen as a worthwhile outcome. There may be other disappointments – try to get them verbalised and expressed.

Body esteem revisited

In Session 21 participants painted an image of themselves entitled, 'Here is an image, painted with love, that shows how I can accept myself'. You kept those paintings, so get them out and use them as the basis for revisiting the subject of body esteem. When we did this section of the programme, we worked hard on trying to get the group to understand where their self-hatred may have come from, the cultural as well as individual pressures, and the value of thinking well of themselves. Revisit where they are with all this now. We would be surprised if their body esteem had not improved. Ask them how it can continue to do so? What do they need to do to continue to improve it? Do they agree that self-hatred serves no useful purpose and only makes it more difficult to feel contented and powerful in their own lives? Are they aware of the way they speak to themselves and can they moderate the critical voice?

Ending

Leave enough time to raise the issue of a three-month follow-up. The idea behind it is to maximise the power of the group by, in effect, keeping it alive in members' minds. The particular focus of this group has been on the replacement of food with people. Keeping those people alive and real in the minds of all the members is probably a useful consolidation of that theme. You, as group leader, will have to feel happy with this idea before you broach it, and of course you will have to be sure that you can book the venue. I would resist all suggestions to have the meeting elsewhere, or for it to take any other form than a group meeting of two hours, like those you have been conducting. There may be pressure for a social meeting, which of course is something that is open to members to arrange for themselves, but this particular follow-up meeting should be formal. Its overt purpose would be to find out how people are doing and support them to continue with the lifestyle change which you have been trying to facilitate. It will also monitor the group's progress on the journey of development on which they have embarked. Ask the group to think about it during the week so that it can be discussed further next week. Stress that it has to be something everyone agrees to, if it is to take place.

Homework

- To be aware of how they talk to themselves about their body and to focus on finding a loving, accepting voice inside them.

Session 35

Time split

- Review — 20 minutes
- Progress report — 60 minutes
- Letters — 25 minutes
- Ending — 15 minutes

Aims and objectives

- To enable group members to review their individual progress over the course of the group and to develop their resolutions for the future via writing and/or painting.
- To introduce the idea of writing letters to other members of the group to use in the final session.
- To devise a group ritual for saying goodbye to be used in the last session.
- To revisit the issue of a follow-up meeting.

Review

The group was asked to focus during the week on how they talk to themselves about their bodies and whether they can find a kind and accepting voice inside themselves. In reviewing how they have done, you may want to refer to the influences from the past which have damaged body esteem, as well as cultural pressures, but focus on encouraging them to recognise their own power to resist and alter these messages. Discuss the futility of self-hatred and the benefits of self-acceptance and self-respect.

Summing up progress and development

The rest of this group is devoted largely to the review of individual progress over the course of the group and the formulation of resolutions or statements about the future. There are lots of ways that you might do this but here are some suggestions.

Suggest that the members review how/whether things have changed for them in the five key areas:

- Awareness of feelings. (Do they know more how they feel; are they able to express those feelings directly in words; are they less likely to turn to food?)
- Self-esteem. (Are they more able to be assertive, recognise what is good for them, act in their own best interests, think well of themselves, like and value themselves?)

- Relationships with others. (How have these changed; are they more able to talk about what is important to them; are they more capable of getting their needs met?)
- Eating behaviour.
- Activity.

Ask people to paint an image of how they are now. This could be done as part of the above exercise or just on its own.

Ask people to write down what has been most important for them about the group, what they have learned, and what they think the most important messages to themselves will be for the future.

As this is now very close to the end of the group, it may be appropriate for the members to share these reflections with each other. Take time to allow each person to share; it can be very useful for other group members.

Group letters and ritual ending

You need to prepare for the last session. My suggestion is that you do two things:

- Ask the members to write a letter during the week to each of the other group members to be distributed in the next session expressing what they have valued in and gained from that person. They don't need to be long and will vary according to how close individuals feel to each other.
- Ask the group to devise a ritual ending for next week. Resist all ideas of turning it into a social occasion with food, etc. It needs to be an occasion which recognises the loss that the ending will bring, as well as what has been gained from the group. You will need to plan it here and now so that any preparations can be made during the week.

Follow-up session

Ask the group whether they have thought about the possibility of a follow-up session in three months' time. Be ready with details of date, time and place, assuming that they will want to do it.

Ending

This is the last ordinary ending you will have with the group. Use it to empower, strengthen, encourage, support as well as to recognise loss.

Homework
- To write letters and prepare for the ritual ending.

Session 36

Time split

- Review   10 minutes
- Letters   45 minutes
- Final consolidation of the message   25 minutes
- Ending   40 minutes

Aims and objectives

- To use the device of letters to enable members to register their appreciation of each other.
- To take a final opportunity to consolidate the messages of the whole group experience.
- To participate in a group ritual to say goodbye.

Review

The review can be brief since you are about to use the letters. Make sure that the ritual ending is agreed and prepared.

Letters

Our experience of using this exercise is that the group members are very touched by the letters they receive. For many of them letters of appreciation will be a new experience. They may be unaware of the qualities that other members have observed in them and pleased to discover that other people have valued them. The hope is that the letters will increase self-esteem and develop trust. They may also be valuable for validating people in the present and for expressing hopes for them for the future.

You will have to think about how exactly you want to do the exercise. How are the letters to be distributed? You might want to suggest that first of all each person reads their letters and then that some of them are shared. You might ask the members to read out the letter that they find most touching/useful/unexpected, etc. These letters have taken time to write, so they should be given time for consideration and appreciation.

Consolidation

When you have spent as much time as seems necessary on the letters, move on to consolidation. This is a final opportunity to distil the essential messages of the whole group. We have provided a list of the group activities for all 36 sessions which you can distribute if you wish (Appendix 11). You might want to do it as a whole group exercise on the flip chart, or get small groups to provide lists and then assemble a master list for the group. If you ask people to identify what has been most important for them – what message will these take away with them – you will probably get an interesting and diverse range of responses.

Ending

Make sure you leave plenty of time for this final ritual ending.

Session	Action
1	Hopes and fears Listening Sharing information
2	Weightline/lifeline Food monitoring Motivational enhancement
3	Strategies for managing overeating Names for feelings Managing feelings
4	Food monitoring Reviewing motivation Feelings in the family Managing feelings
5	Buddying Meal planning Managing feelings
6	Buddying Managing feelings Use of food in your family of origin
7	Meal planning Managing feelings Mothers

8	Mothers
9	Beliefs about food
	Mothers continued
10	Circle of support
	Patchwork mother
11	Who you can trust
	Trusting each other
12	Review of sessions to date
13	Making a menu
	Food choice in family of origin
14	Problem solving for food choice
	Emotional meaning of food choice
15	Goals for food choice
	Shopping for food
16	Food choice
17	Food choice
	Body image and body esteem
18	Fat and thin qualities you value in others
	Qualities you value in yourself
19	Food choice
	Guided fantasy of going to the party
20	If you really loved your body
	Food choice
21	Cultural messages about shape and size
	Image of an acceptable me
22	Progress on weight loss
	Deferring living while waiting for weight loss
23	Positive self-talk
	Body appreciation
24	Review of sessions to date
25	Activity audit
	Emotional eating revisited
26	History of activity
	Food in the family revisited

(Continued)

27	Stepometers Feelings revisited
28	A changing view of their physicality Trust, buddying and relationships revisited
29	Mothers and nurturing revisited
30	Motivation revisited
31	Trust revisited
32	Trust revisited continued Relationships revisited
33	Food choice revisited
34	Hopes and fears revisited Body esteem revisited
35	Progress report letters
36	Letters Final consolidation of the message

PART III
Appendices

Appendix 1

Psychotherapeutic Group for Women who are Seriously Overweight

GROUP CONFIDENTIALITY STATEMENT

During the time that this group will meet, you and your fellow group members are likely to share information about yourselves that is personal and private.

In order to protect yourself and others in the group from this information being disclosed to others outside the group, I would like you to sign the following commitment to confidentiality.

I promise that I will not share what I learn about other people in this group with any other person. I understand that this promise includes sharing information with members of my family.

Signature................................   Date..............................

Name (Print)...

Appendix 2

Outline of the Programme

Weeks 1–12

- All about you and how your history and experience affects your eating behaviour.
- Learning to deal with your feelings without using food.
- Taking better care of yourself.
- Finding and using more support.

Weeks 13–24

- Food choice and how feelings and memories get in the way of making healthy choices.
- How to make better choices.
- Body esteem and how to improve it.

Weeks 25–36

- Activity and how feelings and memories get in the way.
- How to become more active.
- Thinking back about all we did during the programme and making sure it sticks.

Appendix 3

Process of Change

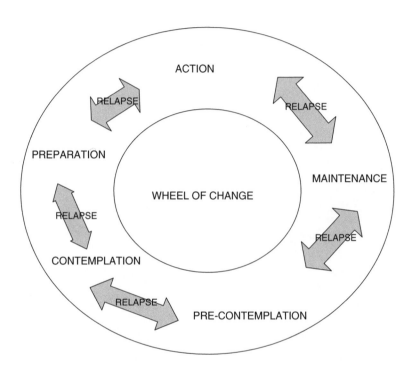

Appendix 4
Food and Mood Sheet

Name.............................. Date..............................

Day..............................

Rating Guide: 1=Lowest rating; 4=Highest rating

Time	Where and with whom?	What did you feel before eating?	What did you feel after eating?	Did you eat more than you wanted?	Hunger rating 1–4	Satisfaction rating 1–4

Appendix 5
How a Child Learns to Manage Feelings

Here is a brief account of how a child in a good situation learns to manage her feelings.

- In the beginning the child's difficult feelings (hunger, pain, anger) are managed by the mother. So, for example, a hungry child who cries is picked up by the mother, soothed and fed. The mother takes in the child's upset feelings and returns them to the child as soothed feelings.

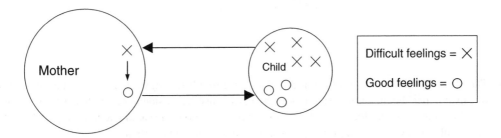

- Over time this system becomes part of the child and enables her to manage her feelings even when the mother is not present. This system continues throughout life once it is firmly in place.

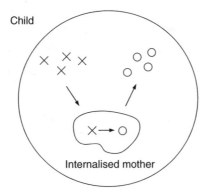

- On the other hand, when early circumstances are not good, the mother is unable to help the child to manage her feelings and may even make things worse. Instead of dealing with her own feelings, the mother is overwhelmed by them. She then feels that the child's feelings are more than she can manage so that she can't turn the child's feelings into good feelings. She may even put her difficult feelings into the child.

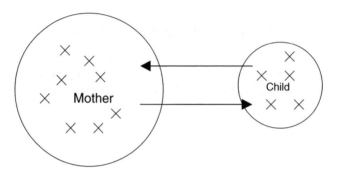

- The effect of this process on the child is that her difficult feelings remain inside her in a kind of capsule that she may not even know is there. She also has inside her a mother who is unable to help her to deal with feelings. The result is a person who is at risk of encountering bad memories without having a good mother inside to help her to manage them.

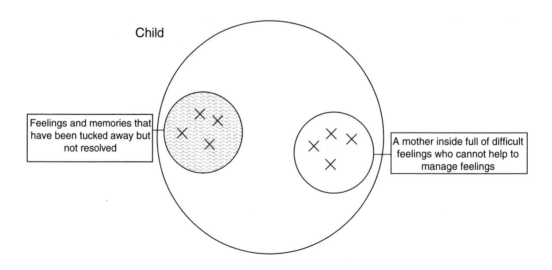

Appendix 6
Meal Planner

Name.............................. Day.............................. Date..............................

Time	Meal/Snack	Details
	Breakfast	
	Snack	
	Lunch	
	Snack	
	Evening meal	
	Snack	

Fill out this form each day with what you plan to eat and when you plan to eat it.

Appendix 7

Questions for 'Food in the Family' Exercise

1. In your situation: who cooked the food or made the meals?

2. What did that person feel about those jobs and in what kind of spirit did they approach them?
   - Did they like them?
   - Did they resent them?
   - Did they feel that that was what they **wanted** to do or what they **had** to do?

3. Who was the food in the family prepared for? Who was the important eater?
   - Was it the children?
   - Was it one of the adults?

4. What do you think the emotional purpose of mealtimes was in your situation?
   - What was supposed to happen there?
   - What was not supposed to happen?
   - Was it an opportunity for everybody to quarrel?
   - Was it an opportunity for the parents to be evil tempered with each other?
   - Was it an opportunity to bully the children?
   - Was it an opportunity to have a nice time together and share the events of the day?
   - Was it an opportunity to say nothing, or to make sure that nothing was said, e.g. by having the television on?

5. Look at your diagram of the room and think about each person in turn.
   - What might each person be saying and to whom?
   - What would be said to you, and what would you say, if anything?
   - Write those things on the diagram.

6. What was your feeling memory of these occasions?
   - What sort of an occasion was it for you?
   - What sorts of things went on that you remember?

7. When you think about all of this, do you think that what went on at mealtimes was a picture of what went on in the family as a whole?
   - Do you think it is an illustration of the relationships in the family?
   - Was that how your family behaved generally?

8. Do you think you had any power?
9. Who did have the power?

Appendix 8

Overview of First 12 Weeks

Session	Action
1	Hopes and fears
	Listening
	Sharing information
2	Weightline/lifeline
	Food monitoring
	Motivational enhancement
3	Strategies for managing overeating
	Names for feelings
	Managing feelings
4	Food monitoring
	Reviewing motivation
	Feelings in the family
	Managing feelings
5	Buddying
	Meal planning
	Managing feelings
6	Buddying
	Managing feelings
	Use of food in your family of origin
7	Meal planning
	Managing feelings
	Mothers
8	Mothers
9	Beliefs about food
	Mothers continued
10	Circle of support
	Patchwork mother
11	Who you can trust
	Trusting each other
12	Review of sessions to date

Appendix 9
Guided Fantasy

Imagine yourself going to a party:

- What image do you want to convey when you get yourself dressed?

- What do you want to convey by the clothes you wear?

- How are you feeling on the way to the party?

- What would you like to happen at the party?

- What are you afraid will happen?

- As you go in to the room you see people looking at you . . . what do you think they are thinking?

- There is food at the party . . . how do you deal with it?

- Someone comes up to you and starts to talk to you and shows that they are attracted to you...how do you respond?

- Is that how you want to respond?

- You see people that you know at the party . . . how do you deal with that?

- People start to dance . . . how do you react?

- It's getting to be time to go home . . . how do you feel?

- You get home and take off your party clothes . . . how do you feel about your body?

- How do you feel about the way you were at the party?

Appendix 10

Overview of First 24 Weeks

Session	Action
1	Hopes and fears Listening Sharing information
2	Weightline/lifeline Food monitoring Motivational enhancement
3	Strategies for managing overeating Names for feelings Managing feelings
4	Food monitoring Reviewing motivation Feelings in the family Managing feelings
5	Buddying Meal planning Managing feelings
6	Buddying Managing feelings Use of food in your family of origin
7	Meal planning Managing feelings Mothers
8	Mothers
9	Beliefs about food Mothers continued
10	Circle of support Patchwork mother
11	Who you can trust Trusting each other
12	Review of sessions to date

13	Making a menu Food choice in family of origin
14	Problem solving for food choice Emotional meaning of food choice
15	Goals for food choice Shopping for food
16	Food choice
17	Food choice Body image and body esteem
18	Fat and thin Qualities you value in others Qualities you value in yourself
19	Food choice Guided fantasy of going to the party
20	If you really loved your body Food choice
21	Cultural messages about shape and size Image of an acceptable me
22	Progress on weight loss Deferring living while waiting for weight loss
23	Positive self-talk Body appreciation
24	Review of sessions to date

Appendix 11
Overview of Entire 36 Weeks

Session	Action
1	Hopes and fears Listening Sharing information
2	Weightline/lifeline Food monitoring Motivational enhancement
3	Strategies for managing overeating Names for feelings Managing feelings
4	Food monitoring Reviewing motivation Feelings in the family Managing feelings
5	Buddying Meal planning Managing feelings
6	Buddying Managing feelings Use of food in your family of origin
7	Meal planning Managing feelings Mothers
8	Mothers
9	Beliefs about food Mothers continued
10	Circle of support Patchwork mother
11	Who you can trust Trusting each other
12	Review of sessions to date

13	Making a menu Food choice in family of origin
14	Problem solving for food choice Emotional meaning of food choice
15	Goals for food choice Shopping for food
16	Food choice
17	Food choice Body image and body esteem
18	Fat and thin Qualities you value in others Qualities you value in yourself
19	Food choice Guided fantasy of going to the party
20	If you really loved your body Food choice
21	Cultural messages about shape and size Image of an acceptable me
22	Progress on weight loss Deferring living while waiting for weight loss
23	Positive self-talk Body appreciation
24	Review of sessions to date
25	Activity audit Emotional eating revisited
26	History of activity Food in the family revisited
27	Stepometers Feelings revisited
28	A changing view of their physicality Trust, buddying and relationships revisited
29	Mothers and nurturing revisited
30	Motivation revisited
31	Trust revisited
32	Trust revisited continued Relationships revisited

33	Food choice revisited
34	Hopes and fears revisited Body esteem revisited
35	Progress report Letters
36	Letters Final consolidation of the message

References

ACSM (American College of Sports Medicine) (1995) *ACSM's Guidelines for Exercise Testing and Prescription.* Philadelphia: Williams & Wilkins.

Addis, M.E. & Mahalik, J.R. (2003) Men, masculinity and the contexts of help-seeking. *American Psychologist*, **58**, 5–14.

Agras, W.S., Telch, C.F., Arnow, B.A., Eldredge, K. & Marnell, M. (1997) One year follow-up of cognitive-behavioural therapy for obese individuals with binge eating disorder. *Journal of Consulting and Clinical Psychology*, **65**, 343–347.

Alexander, P.N. (1998) A comparison of employee assistance program client satisfaction based on supervisory referral versus self-referral. *The Sciences and Engineering*, **59**, 6-B, 2675.

Arnow, B., Kenardy, J. & Agras, W.S. (1995) The Emotional Eating Scale: The Development of a Measure to Assess Coping with Negative Affect by Eating. *International Journal of Eating Disorders*, **18** (1), 79–90.

Aveline, M. & Dryden, W. (1988) Group Therapy in Britain: An introduction. In Aveline, M. and Dryden, W. (eds) *Group Therapy in Britain.* Milton Keynes: OUP, 1–10.

Bandura, A. (1997) *Self-efficacy: The Exercise of Control.* New York: W.H. Freeman.

Benjamin, O. & Kamin-Shaaltiel, S. (2004) It's not because I'm fat: Perceived overweight and anger avoidance in marriage. *Health Care for Women International*, **25** (9), 853–871.

Benson, J.F. (2001) *Working More Creatively with Groups.* London: Routledge.

Bidgood, J. & Buckroyd, J. (2005) An exploration of obese adults experience of attempting to lose weight and to maintain a reduced weight. *Counselling and Psychotherapy Research*, **5** (3), 221–229.

Blackburn, G.L. (2002) Weight loss and risk factors. In Fairburn, C.G. and Brownell, K.D. (eds) *Eating Disorders and Obesity. A Comprehensive Handbook* (2nd edition). New York: Guilford Press.

Blair, S.N. & Connelly, J.C. (1996) How much physical activity should we do? The case for moderate amounts and intensities of physical activity. *Research Quarterly for Exercise and Sport*, **67** (2), 193–205.

Bloom, C., Gitter, A., Gutwill, S., Kogel, L. & Zaphiropoulos, L. (1999) The truth about dieting: A feminist view. In Lemberg, R. and Cohn, L. (eds) *Eating Disorders: A Reference Sourcebook* (61–64). Phoenix: Oryx.

Bowlby, J. (2000a) *Attachment.* London: Basic Books.

Bowlby, J. (2000b) *Separation.* London: Basic Books.

Bowlby, J. (2000c) *Loss.* London: Basic Books.

British Association for Counselling and Psychotherapy. www.bacp.co.uk/education/whatiscounselling.html

Brodney, S., Blair, S.N. & Lee, C.D. (2000) Is it possible to be overweight or obese and fit and healthy? In Bouchard, C. (ed.) *Physical Activity and Obesity.* Champaign, IL: Human Kinetics.

Brownell, K.D. & Wadden, T.A. (1992) Etiology and treatment of obesity: Understanding a serious, prevalent and refractory disorder. *Journal of Consulting and Clinical Psychology*, **60**, 505–517.

Buckroyd, J. (1994) Eating disorders as psychosomatic illness: The implications for treatment. *Psychodynamic Counselling*, **1** (1), 106–118.

Buckroyd, J., Rother, S. & Stott, D. (2006) Weight loss as a primary objective of therapeutic groups for obese women: Two preliminary studies. *British Journal of Guidance and Counselling*, **34** (2), 245–265.

Buckroyd, J. & Rother, S. (in prep. a) Recruitment for weight management groups for obese women: Referral or self-referral?

Buckroyd, J., Green, G. & Rother, S. (in prep. b) Disordered eating cognitions and behaviours among slimming organisation competition winners.

Buckroyd, J., Rother, S., Ellis, V. & Seamoore, D. (in prep. c) Developing interventions to treat obesity: Women's perceptions of the emotional factors contributing to their obesity.

Burgard, D. & Lyons, P. (1994) Alternatives in obesity treatment: Focusing on health for fat women. In Fallon, P., Katzman, M.A. and Wooley, S.C. (eds) *Feminist Perspectives on Eating Disorders*. New York: Guilford Press.

Byrne, S.M., Cooper, Z. & Fairburn, C.G. (2003) Weight maintenance and relapse in obesity: a qualitative study. *International Journal of Obesity*, **27**, 955–962.

Byrne, S.M., Cooper, Z. & Fairburn, C.G. (2004) Psychological predictors of weight regain in obesity. *Behaviour, Research and Therapy*, **42** (11), 1341–1356.

Canetti, L., Bachar, E. & Berry, E.M. (2002) Food and emotion. *Behavioural Processes*, **60** (2), 1–10.

Carrier, K.M., Steinhardt, M.A. & Bowman, S. (1994) Rethinking traditional weight management programs: A 3-year follow-up evaluation of a new approach. *Journal of Psychology*, **128**, 517–535.

Carryer, J. (2001) Embodied largeness: A significant women's health issue. *Nursing Inquiry*, **8**, 90–97.

Chagnon, Y.C., Rankinen, T., Snyder, E.E., Weisnagel, S.J., Perusse, L., & Bouchard, C. (2003) The human obesity gene map: the 2002 update. *Obesity Research*, **11**, 313–367.

Chua, J.L., Touyz, S. & Hill, A.J. (2004). Negative mood-induced overeating in obese binge eaters: An experimental study. *International Journal of Obesity and Related Metabolic Disorders*, **28** (4), 606–610.

Ciarrochi, J. & Scott, G. (2006) The link between emotional competence and well-being: A longitudinal study. *British Journal of Guidance and Counselling*, **34** (2), 231–243.

Ciechanowski, P., Russo, J., Katon, W., Von Korff, M., Ludman, E., Lin, E., Simon, G. & Bush, T. (2004) Influence of patient attachment style on self-care and outcomes in diabetes. *Psychosomatic Medicine*, **66**, 720–728.

Ciliska, D. (1998) Evaluation of Two Nondieting Interventions for Obese Women. *Western Journal of Nursing Research*, **20**, 119–135.

Clark, M. & Hampson, S.E. (2001) Implementing a psychological intervention to improve lifestyle self-management in patients with Type 2 diabetes. *Patient Education and Counselling*, **42** (3), 247–256.

Clerici, M., Albonetti, S., Papa, R., Renati, G. & Invernizzi, G. (1992) Alexithymia and Obesity. *Psychotherapy and Psychosomatics*, **57**, 88–93.

Cochrane, C., Brewerton, T., Wilson, D. & Hodges, E. (1993) Alexithymia in the eating disorders. *International Journal of Eating Disorders*, **14**: 219–222.

Cogan, J. & Ernsberger, P. (1999) Dieting, Weight and Health: Reconceptualizing Research and Policy. *Journal of Social Issues*, **55** (2), 187–205.

Cognolato, S., Silvestri, A., Fiorellini Bernardis, A.L. & Santonastaso, P. (1996) Psychodynamic group psychotherapy with obese patients. *Minerva Psichiatrica*, **37** (1), 5–12.

Colantuoni, C., Rada, P., McCarthy, J., Patten, C., Avena, N.M., Chadeayne, A. & Hoebel, B.G. (2002) Evidence that intermittent, excessive sugar intake causes endogenous opioid dependency. *Behaviour Modification*, **27**, 478–488.

Collins, P. & Williams, G. (2001) Drug treatment of Obesity: from past failures to future successes? *British Journal of Clinical Pharmacology*, **51**, 13–25.

Colvin, R.H. & Olson, S.B. (1983) A descriptive analysis of men and women who have lost significant weight and are highly successful at maintaining the loss. *Addictive Behaviors*, **8**, 287–295.

Conner, M. & Armitage, C.J. (2002) *The Social Psychology of Food*. Buckingham: Open University Press.

Conway, B. & Rene, A. (2004) Obesity as a disease: no lightweight matter. ***Obesity*** Reviews, **5**, 145–51.

Cooper, Z., Fairburn, C.G. & Hawker, D.M. (2003) *Cognitive Behavioral Treatment of Obesity: A Clinician's Guide*. New York: Guilford Press.

Crisp, A.H. (1988) Social and psychopathological aspects of obesity in James, W.P.T. and Parker, S.W. (eds) *Current Approaches: Obesity*. Duphar Medical Relations, 29–41.

Dallman, M.F., Pecoraro, N.C. & la Fleur, S.E. (2005) Chronic stress and comfort foods: Self-medication and abdominal obesity. *Brain, Behavior and Immunity*, **19**, 275–280.

Davis, E., Rovi, S. & Johnson, M.S. (2005). Mental Health, Family Function and Obesity in African American Women. *Journal of the National Medical Association*, **97**, 478–482.

Deaver, C.M., Miltenberger, R.G., Smyth, J., Meidinger, A. & Crosby, R. (2003) An Evaluation of Affect and Binge Eating. *Behaviour Modification*, **27** (4), 578–599.

De Chouly De Lenclave, M.B., Florequin, C. & Bailly, D. (2001) Obesity, alexithymia, psychopathology and binge eating: a comparative study of 40 obese patients and 32 controls. *Encephale*, **27**, 343–350.

Department of Health (DOH) (2004) *Choosing Health: Making healthy choices easier. Executive Summary*, London, U.K.: H. M. Government.

Després, J.-P., Golay, A. Sjöström, L. (2005) Effects of Rimonabant on Metabolic Risk Factors in Overweight Patients with Dyslipidemia. *The New England Journal of Medicine*, **353** (20), 2121–2134.

Devlin, M.J., Walsh, B.T., Spitzer, R.L. & Hasin, D. (1992) Is there another binge eating disorder? A review of literature on overeating in the absence of bulimia nervosa. *International Journal of Eating Disorders*, **11**, 333–340.

Devlin, M.J. (2001) Binge-eating disorder and obesity. A combined treatment approach. *Psychiatric Clinics of North America*, **24** (2), 325–35.

De Zwaan, M., Bach, M., Mitchell, J.E., Ackard, D., Specker, S.M., Pyle, R.L., Pakesch, G. (1995) Alexithymia, obesity and binge eating disorder. *International Journal of Eating Disorders*, **17**, 135–140.

Dokter, D. (Ed.) (1994) *Arts Therapies and Clients with Eating Disorders*. London: Jessica Kingsley Publishers.

Douketis, J.D., Feightner, J.W., Attia, J. & Feldman, W.F. (1999) Periodic health examination, 1999 update: 1. Detection, prevention and treatment of obesity. *Canadian Medical Association Journal*, **160**, 513–525.

Eberhardt, M.S., Ogden, C. & Engelgau, M., Cadwell, B. (2004) Prevalence of overweight and obesity among adults with diagnosed diabetes. *Morbidity and Mortality Weekly Report*, **53**, 1066–1068.

Egolf, B., Lasker, L., Wolf, S. & Potvin, L. (1992) The Roseto Effect: A 50-year comparison of mortality rates. *American Journal of Public Health*, **82**, 1089–92.

Eldredge, K.L. & Agras, W.S. (1996) Weight and shape overconcern and emotional eating in binge eating disorder. *International Journal of Eating Disorders*, **19**, 73–82.

Elfhag, K., Carlsson, A.M. & Rössner, S. (2003) Subgrouping in obesity based on Rorschach personality characteristics. *Scandinavian Journal of Psychology*, **44** (5), 399–407.

Encinosa, W.E., Bernard, D.M., Chen, C-C. & Steiner, C.A. (2006) Healthcare Utilization and Outcomes After Bariatric Surgery. *Medical Care*, **44** (8), 706–712.

Epel, E., Lapidus, R., McEwen, B. & Brownell, K. (2001) Stress may add bite to appetite in women: a laboratory study of stress-induced cortisol and eating behaviour. *Psychoneuroendocrinology*, **26**, 37–49.

Evans, C., Mellor-Clark, J., Margison, F., Barkham, M., Audin, K., Connell, J. & McGrath, G. (2000) CORE: Clinical Outcomes in Routine Evaluation. *Journal of Mental Health*, **9** (3), 247–255.

Fabricatore, A.N. & Wadden, T.A. (2004) Psychological Aspects of Obesity. *Clinics in Dermatology*, **22**, 332–337.

Fairburn, C.G., Doll, H.A., Welch, S.L., Hay, P.J., Davies, B.A. & O'Connor, M.E. (1998) Risk Factors for Binge Eating Disorders. *Archives of General Psychiatry*, **55**, 425–432.

Fallon, P., Katzman, M.A. & Wooley, S.C. (eds) (1994) *Feminist Perspectives on Eating Disorders*. New York, NY: The Guilford Press.

Felitti, V.J. (1991) Long-term medical consequences of incest, rape and molestation. *Southern Medical Journal*, **84** (3), 328–31.

Felitti, V.J. (1993) Childhood sexual abuse, depression and family dysfunction in adult obese patients: a case control study. *Southern Medical Journal*, **86** (7), 732–6.

Felitti, V.J., Anda, R.F., Nordenberg, D., Williamson, D.F., Spitz, A.M., Edwards, V., Koss, M.P. & Marks, J.S. (1998) Relationship of childhood abuse and household dysfunction to many of the leading causes of death in adults. *American Journal of Preventive Medicine*, **14**, 245–258.

Felitti, V.J. (2003). The Origins of Addiction: Evidence from the Adverse Childhood Experiences Study [www document] http://acestudy.org/docs/OriginsofAddiction.pdf [Accessed 3/5/06]. English version of the article published in Germany as: Felitti, V.J. (2003). Ursprünge des Suchtverhaltens – Evidenzen aus einer Studie zu belastenden Kindheitserfahrungen. *Praxis der Kinderpsychologie und Kinderpsychiatrie*, **52**, 547–559.

Fichter, M.M., Quadflieg, N. & Brandl, B. (1993) Recurrent overeating: An empirical comparison of binge eating disorder, bulimia and obesity. *International Journal of Eating Disorders*, **14**, 1–16.

Field, A.E., Baenoya, J. & Colditz, G.A. (2002). Epidemiology and Health and Economic Consequences of Obesity. In Wadden, T.A. and Stunkard, A.J. (eds) *Handbook of Obesity Treatment*. New York: The Guilford Press.

Flores, P.J. (2001) Addiction as an Attachment Disorder: Implication Therapy. *International Journal of Group Psychotherapy*, **51** (1), 63–81.

Forbes, D. (1994) *False Fixes: The cultural politics of drugs, alcohol and addictive relationships*. Albany: State University of New York Press.

Foreyt, J.P. & Goodrick, G.K. (1994) Attributes of successful approaches to weight loss and control. *Applied and Preventive Psychology*, **3**, 209–215.

Foster, G.D. & Kendall, P.C. (1994) The realistic treatment of obesity: Changing the scales of success. *Clinical Psychology Review*, **14**, 701–736.

Freeman, L.M. & Gil, K.M. (2004) Daily stress, coping and dietary restraint in binge eating. *International Journal of Eating Disorders*, **36**, 204–212.

Friedman, M.A. & Brownell, K.D. (2002) Psychological Consequences of Obesity. In Fairburn, C.G. and Brownell, K.D. (eds) *Eating Disorders and Obesity*. New York: The Guilford Press.

Frothingham, T.E., Hobbs, C.J., Wynne, J.M., Yee, L., Goyal, A. & Wadsworth, D.J. (2000) Follow up study eight years after diagnosis of sexual abuse. *Archives of Disease in Childhood*, **83**, 132–134.

Garland, J., Jones, H. & Kolodny, K. (1965) A model for stages in the development of social work groups in Bernstein, S. (ed) *Explorations in Group Work*. London: Bookstall.

Garner, D.M. & Wooley, S.C. (1991) Confronting the failure of behavioural and dietary treatments for obesity. *Clinical Psychology Review*, **11**, 729–780.

Geliebter, A. & Aversa, A. (2003) Emotional eating in overweight, normal weight and underweight individuals. *Eating Behaviors*, **3** (4), 341–347.

George, C., Kaplan, N. & Main, M. (1996) *Adult Attachment Interview*. Unpublished manuscript, Department of Psychology, University of California, Berkeley (third edition).

Gerhardt, S. (2004) *Why Love Matters: How Affection Shapes a Baby's Brain*. Hove: Brunner Routledge.

Gilbert, S. (2000) *Counselling for Eating Disorders*. London: Sage Publications Ltd.

Glenny, A. & O'Meara, S. (1997) Systematic Review of Interventions in the Treatment and Prevention of Obesity. York: NHS Centre for Reviews and Dissemination, Report 10.

Gluck, M.E., Geliebter, A. & Lorence, M. (2004) Cortisol Stress Response is Positively Correlated with Central Obesity in Obese Women with Binge Eating Disorder (BED) before and after Cognitive-Behavioral Treatment. *Annals of the New York Academy of Sciences*, **1032**, 202–207.

Goleman, D. (1995) *Emotional Intelligence*. USA: Bantam Books.

Goodrick, G.K., Pendleton, V.R. & Kimball, K.T. Carlos Poston, W.S., Reeves, R.S., Foreyt, J.P. (1999) Binge eating severity self-concept, dieting self-efficacy and social support during treatment of binge eating disorder. *International Journal of Eating Disorders*, **26**, 295.

Goodspeed-Grant, P. & Boersma, H. (2005) Making sense of being fat: A hermeneutic analysis of adults' explanations for obesity. *Counselling and Psychotherapy Research*, **5** (3), 212–220.

Goran, M.I., Gower, B.A., Nagy, T.R. & Johnson, R.K. (1998) Developmental Changes in Energy Expenditure and Physical Activity in Children: Evidence for a Decline in Physical Activity in Girls Before Puberty. *Pediatrics*, **101**, 887–891.

Gormally, J., Rardin, D. & Black, S. (1980) Correlates of successful response to a behavioural weight control clinic. *Journal of Counseling Psychology*, **27**, 179–191.

Gormally, J., Black, S., Daston, S. & Rardin, D. (1982) The assessment of binge eating severity among obese persons. *Addictive Behaviours*, **7**, 47–55.

Grilo, C.M. & Masheb, R.M. (2001) Childhood Psychological, Physical and Sexual Maltreatment in outpatients with Binge Eating Disorder: Frequency and Associations with Gender, Obesity and Eating-Related Psychopathology. *Obesity Research*, **9**, 320–325.

Grilo, C.M., Masheb, R.M., Brody, M., Toth, C., Burke-Martindale, C. & Rothschild, B. (2005) Childhood Maltreatment in Extremely Obese Male and Female Bariatric Surgery Candidates. *Obesity Research*, **13** (1), 123–130.

Gustafson T.B. & Sarwer D.B. (2004). Childhood sexual abuse and obesity. *Obesity Reviews*, **5**, 129–135.

Hartford, M.E. (1972) *Groups in Social Work: Application of Small Group Theory and Research to Social Work Practice*. New York: Columbia University Press.

Harvey, E.L., Glenny, A.M., Kirk, S.F.L. & Summerbell, C.D. (2002) An updated systematic review of interventions to improve health professionals' management of obesity. *Obesity Reviews*, **3**, 45.

Harvey E.L., Glenny A.M., Kirk S.F.L., Summerbell C.D. (2002a) Improving health professionals' management and the organisation of care for overweight and obese people (Cochrane Review). In: *The Cochrane Library*, Issue 4. Oxford: Update Software.

Haslam, D.W. & James, W.P.T. (2005) Obesity. *Lancet* **366**, 1197–1209.

Hay, P.J., Bacaltchuk, J. & Stefano, S. (2004) Psychotherapy for bulimia nervosa and binging. *Cochrane Database of Systematic Reviews*, Issue 3. Art. No.: CD000562.DOI: 10.1002/14651858. CD000562.pub2.

Hayaki, J., Brownell K. (1996) Behaviour change in practice: group approaches. *International Journal of Obesity*, **20** (1), S27–30.

Hayward, L.M., Nixon, C., Jasper, M.P., Murphy, K.M., Harlan, V., Swirda, L. & Hayward, K. (2000) The process of restructuring and the treatment of obesity in women. *Health Care for Women International*, **21**, 615–630.

Heatherton, T.F. & Baumeister R.F. (1991) Binge eating as escape from self-awareness. *Psychological Bulletin*, **110**, 86–108.

Heenan, C. (2005) A feminist psychotherapeutic approach to working with women who eat compulsively. *Counselling and Psychotherapy Research*, **5** (3), 238–45.

Heiat, A. (2003) Impact of Age on Definition of Standards for Ideal Weight. *Preventive Cardiology*, **6**, 104–107.

Heinrichs, M., Baumgartner, T., Kirschbaum, C. & Ehlert, U. (2003). Social support and oxytocin interact to suppress cortisol and subjective responses to psychosocial stress. *Biological Psychiatry*, **54**, 1389–1398.

Herman, J.L. (1992) *Trauma and Recovery*. USA: Basic Books.

Hinz, L.D. (2006) *Drawing from Within: Using Art to Treat Eating Disorders*. London: Jessica Kingsley Publishers.

Hodge, J. (1997) Social groupwork: rules for establishing the group. *Social Work Today*, **8** (17), 110.

Holmes, J. (2003) *John Bowlby and Attachment Theory*. Hove: Brunner Routledge.

Hoppe, R. & Ogden, J. (1997) Practice nurses' beliefs about obesity and weight related interventions in primary care. *International Journal of Obesity and Related Metabolic Disorders*, **21** (2), 141–146.

House of Commons Health Committee (2004) *Obesity: Third Report of Session 2003–04*. London: The Stationery Office.

Howe, D. (2003) Attachment and Human Development. *Psychology Press*, **5** (3), 265–270.

Hulme, P.A. (2004) Theoretical Perspectives on the Health Problems of Adults who Experienced Childhood Sexual Abuse. *Issues in Mental Health Nursing*, **25** (4), 339–361.

Hyde, K. (1988) Analytic Group Psychotherapies. In Aveline, M. and Dryden, W. (eds) *Group Therapy in Britain*. Milton Keynes: OUP, 13–42.

James, O. (2007) *Affluenza – How to be successful and stay sane*. London: Vermilion.

James, P.T., Astrup, A., Finer, N., Hilsted, J., Kopelman, P., Rössner, S., Saris, W.H.M., Van Gaal, L.F. (2000) Effect of sibutramine on weight maintenance after weight loss: a randomised trial. *The Lancet*, **356**, Issue 9248, 2119–2125.

Jeffery, R.W., Bjornson-Benson, W.M., Rosenthal, B.S., Lindquist, R.A., Kurth, C.L. & Johnson, S.L. (1984) Correlates of Weight Loss and Its Maintenance over Two Years of Follow-Up among Middle-Aged Men. *Preventive Medicine*, **13**, 155–168.

Jeffery, R.W., Drewnowski, A., Epstein, L.H., Stunkard, A.J., Wilson, G.T., Wing, R.R. & Hill, D.R. (2000) Long-Term Maintenance of Weight Loss: Current Status. *Health Psychology*, **19** (1) (Suppl.) 5–16.

Jia, H., Li, J.Z., Leserman, J., Hu, Y. & Drossman, D. (2004). Relationship of Abuse History and Other Risk Factors with Obesity Among Female Gastrointestinal Patients. *Digestive Diseases and Sciences*, **49** (5), 872–877.

Kahn, M. (1997) *Between Therapist and Client: The New Relationship*. Revised edition. US: Freeman.

Kasila, K., Poskiparta, M., Karhila, P. & Kettunen, T. (2003) Patients' readiness for dietary change at the beginning of counselling: a transtheoretical model-based assessment. *Journal of Human Nutrition and Dietetics*, **16**, 159–166.

Kasser, T. (2002) *The High Price of Materialism*. Cambridge, Massachusetts: The MIT Press.

Kenardy, J., Arnow, B. & Agras W.S. (1996) The aversiveness of specific emotional states associated with binge-eating in obese subjects. *Australia and New Zealand Journal of Psychiatry*, **30** (6), 839–844.

Kendall-Tackett, K. (2002). The Health Effects of Childhood Abuse: Four Pathways by which Abuse Can Influence Health. *Child Abuse and Neglect*, **6** (7), 715–730.

Kent, A., Waller, G. & Dagnan, D. (1999) A greater role of emotional than physical or sexual abuse in predicting disordered eating attitudes: The role of mediating variables. *International Journal of Eating Disorders*, **25** (2), 159–167.

Kern, L.S., Friedman, K., Rechmann, S.K., Costanzo, P.R. & Musante, G.J. (2002) Changing eating behaviour: A preliminary study to consider broader measures of weight control treatment success. *Eating Behaviors*, **3** (2), 113.

King, A.C., Taylor, C.B., Haskell, W.L. & Debusk, R.F. (1988) Strategies for Increasing Early Adherence to and Long-Term Mintenance of Home-Based Exercise Training in Healthy Middle-Aged Men and Women. *American Journal of Cardiology*, **61** (6), 28–32.

King, T.K., Clark, M.M. & Pera, V. (1996). History of sexual abuse and obesity treatment outcome. *Addictive Behaviours*, **21** (3), 283–290.

Klem, M.L., Wing, R.R., McGuire, M.T., Seagle, H.M. & Hill, J.O. (1997) A descriptive study of individuals successful at long-term maintenance of substantial weight loss. *American Journal of Clinical Nursing*, **66**, 239–246.

Kohut, H. (1984) *How Does Analysis Cure?* Chicago: University of Chicago Press.

Kopp, W. (1994). The incidence of sexual abuse in women with eating disorders. *Psychotherapie, Psychosomatik, Medizinische Psychologie*, **44** (5), 159–162.

Latner, J.D. (2001) Self-help in the long-term treatment of obesity. *Obesity Reviews*, **2**, 87–97.

Lawrence, M. & Dana, M. (1990) *Fighting Food: Coping with Eating Disorders*. London, UK: Penguin Books Ltd.

Lean, M.E.J. (2005) Prognosis in obesity. *BMJ*, **330**, 1339–40.

Leather, S. (2003) Social inequalities, nutrition and obesity. In Voss, L.D. and Wilkin, T.J. (eds) *Adult Obesity: A paediatric challenge*. London, UK: Taylor and Francis, 53–60.

Lee, L. & Shapiro, C.M. (2003) Psychological manifestations of obesity. *Journal of Psychosomatic Research*, **55** (6), 477–479.

Leserman, J. (2005) Sexual Abuse History: Prevalence, Health Effects, Mediators, and Psychological Treatment. *Psychosomatic Medicine*, **67**, 906–915.

Lessem, P.A. (2005) *Self Psychology: An Introduction*. Maryland: Jason Aronson.

Lewis, V.J., Blair, A.J. & Booth, D.A. (1992) Outcome of Group Therapy for Body-Image Emotionality and Weight-Control Self-Efficacy. *Behavioural Psychotherapy*, **20**, 155–165.

Liebbrand, R. & Fichter, M.M. (2002) Maintenance of weight loss after obesity treatment: is continuous support necessary? *Behaviour Research and Therapy*, **40**, 1275–1289.

Linde, J.A., Jeffrey, R.W., Levy, R.L., Sherwood, N.E., Utter, J., Pronk, N.P. & Boyle, R.G. (2004) Binge eating disorder, weight control self-efficacy, and depression in overweight men and women. *International Journal of Obesity and Related Metabolic Disorders*, **28** (3), 418–425.

Lissau, I. & Sotrensen, T.I.A. (1994) Parental neglect during childhood and increased risk of obesity in young adulthood. *Lancet*, **343**, 324–7.

Logue, A.W. (2004) *The Psychology of Eating and Drinking.* New York: Brunner Routledge.

Logue, E., Sutton, K., Jarjoura, D. & Smucker, W. (2000) Obesity management in primary care: assessment of readiness to change among 284 family practice patients. *Journal of the American Board of Family Practitioners*, **13**, 164–171.

Loneck, B., Garrett, J.A. & Banks, S.M. (1996) A comparison of the Johnson intervention with four other methods of referral to outpatient treatment. *American Journal of Drug and Alcohol Abuse*, **22**.

Lowe, M.R. & Levine, A.S. (2005) Eating Motives and the Controversy over Dieting: Eating Less Than Needed versus Less Than Wanted. *Obesity Research*, **13**, 797–806.

Lyons, M.A. (1998) The phenomenon of compulsive overeating in a selected group of professional women. *Journal of Advanced Nursing*, **27**, 1158–64.

MacMillan, H.L., Fleming, J.E., Streiner, D.L., Lin, E., Boyle, M.H., Jamieson, E., Duku, E.K., Walsh, C.A., Wong, M.Y.Y. & Beardslee, W.R. (2001). Childhood Abuse and Lifetime Psychopathology in a Community Sample. *American Journal of Psychiatry*, **158**, 1878–1883.

Maiese, D.R. (2002) Healthy People 2010-Leading Health Indicators for Women. *Women's Health Issues*, **12**, (4) 155–164.

Manson, J.E., Greenland, P.H.P., Lacroix, A.Z., Stefanick, M.L., Mouton, C.P., Oberman, A., Perri, M.G., Sheps, D.S., Pettinger, M.B. & Siscovick, D.S. (2002) Walking Compared with Vigorous Exercise for the Prevention of Cardiovascular Events in Women. *The New England Journal of Medicine*, **347**, 716–725.

Marcus, M.D. & Wing, R.R. (1987) Binge eating among the obese. *Annals of Behavioural Medicine*, **9**, 23–37.

Matsakis, A. (1994) *Post-traumatic stress disorder: A complete treatment guide.* Oakland, California: New Harbinger Publications.

Maunder, R. & Hunter, J. (2001) Attachment and Psychosomatic Medicine: Developmental Contributions to Stress and Disease. *Psychosomatic Medicine*, **63**, 556–567.

McElroy, M. (2002) *Resistance to Exercise: A Social Analysis of Inactivity.* Champaign: Human Kinetics.

McFarlane, T., Polivy, J. & McCabe, R.E. (1999) Help, Not Harm: Psychological Foundation for a Nondieting Approach Toward Health. *Journal of Social Issues*, **55**, 261–276.

McKisack, C. & Waller, G. (1997) Factors Influencing the Outcome of Group Psychotherapy for Bulimia Nervosa. *International Journal of Eating Disorders*, **22**, 1–13.

Miller, W.C., Koceja, D.M. & Hamilton, E.J. (1997) A meta-analysis of the past 25 years of weight loss research using diet, exercise or diet plus exercise intervention. *International Journal of Obesity*, **21** (10), 941–947.

Mills, J.K. (1995) A note on interpersonal sensitivity and psychotic symptomatology in obese adult outpatients with a history of childhood obesity. *Journal of Psychology*, **129**, 345–348.

Mitchell, J.E. & Courcoulas A.P. (2005) Overview of Bariatric Surgery Procedures. In Mitchell, J.E. and Zwaan, M. de (eds) *Bariatric Surgery: A Guide for Mental Health Professionals.* New York: Routledge.

Möller-Leimkühler, A.M. (2000) Barriers to help-seeking by men: a review of sociocultural and clinical literature with particular reference to depression. *Journal of Affective Disorders*, **71**, 1–9.

Mollon, P. (1996) *Multiple selves, multiple voices: working with trauma, violation and dissociation*. London: Wiley Publishers.

Mollon, P. (2001) *Releasing the Self: The Healing Legacy of Heinz Kohut*. London: Whurr.

Morris, J.N. & Hardman, A.E. (1997) Walking in health. *Sports Medicine*, **23**, 306–332.

Morrison, A.L. (1999) The effects of alternative group interventions on physical self-esteem in obese women. *Dissertation Abstracts International Section A:-Humanities and Social Sciences*, **59** (9A), 3361.

National Institutes of Health (2000) The practical guide: Identification, evaluation and treatment of overweight and obesity in adults. *U.S. Department of Health and Human Services. NIH Publication No. 00-4084*.

NIHCE guidelines (2006) Obesity: the prevention, identification, assessment and management of overweight and obesity in adults and children.

NHLBI (National Heart, Lung and Blood Institute). Obesity Education Initiative Expert Panel (1998) Clinical guidelines on the identification, evaluation and treatment of overweight and obesity in adults-The evidence report. *Obesity Research*, **6**, 51S–210S.

NHS Modernisation Agency/NHS Alliance (2005) Commissioning Obesity Services. Northumbria, Primary Care Development Centre: Northumbria University.

O'Brien, M.O. & Houston, G. (2000) *Integrative Therapy: A practitioner's guide*. London: Sage Publications Ltd.

Ogden, J. (1998) The role of family status and ethnic group on body image and eating behaviour. *International Journal of Eating Disorders*, **23**, 309–315.

Ogden, J. (2000) The role of the mother-daughter relationship in explaining weight concern. *International Journal of Eating Disorders*, **28**, 78–83.

Ogden, J. (2003) *The psychology of eating*. Oxford: Blackwell Publishing.

Omaha, J. (2004) http://www.bestmindhealth.com/library/2004-11-14e.html accessed 30/10/2006.

O'Meara, S., Riemsma, R., Shirran, L., Mather, L. & Ter Riet, G. (2001) A rapid and systematic review of the clinical effectiveness and cost-effectiveness of orlistat in the management of obesity. *Health Technology Assessment*, **5**, 1–81.

O'Meara, S.O., Riemsma, R., Shirran, L., Mather, L. & Ter Riet, G. (2004) A systematic review of the clinical effectiveness of orlistat used for the management of obesity. *Obesity Reviews*, **5**, 51.

Omichinski, L. & Harrison, K.R. (1995) Reduction of Dieting Attitudes and Practises after Participation in a Non-Diet Lifestyle Program. *Journal of the Canadian Dietetic Association*, 56.

Orbach, S. (1978) *Fat is a Feminist Issue*. London, UK: Arrow.

Orford, J. (2001) *Excessive Appetites: A Psychological View of Addictions*. 2nd Edition. Chichester: John Wiley & Sons Ltd.

Parsons, T., Power, C., Logan, S. & Summerbell, C. (1999) Childhood predictors of adult obesity: a systematic review. *International Journal of Obesity*, **23** (8), 1–107.

Pendleton, V.R., Goodrick, G.K., Carlos Poston, W.S., Reeves, R.S. & Foreyt, J.P. (2002) Exercise Augments the Effects of Cognitive-Behavioral Therapy in the Treatment of Binge Eating. *International Journal of Eating Disorders*, **31**, 172–184.

Perri, M.G., McAllister, D.A., Gange, J.J., Jordan, R.C., McAdoo, W.G. & Nezu, A.M. (1988) Effects of four maintenance programmes on the long term management of obesity. *Journal of Consulting and Clinical Psychology*, **56**, 529–534.

Perri, M.G., Nezu, A.M. & Viegener, B.J. (1992) *Improving the long-term management of obesity: theory, research and clinical guidelines*. New York: Wiley.

Perri, M.G., Martin, A.D., Notelovitz, M., Leermakers, E.A. & Sears, S.F. (1997) Effects of Group- versus Home-Based Exercise in the Treatment of Obesity. *Journal of Consulting and Clinical Psychology*, **65**, 278–285.

Perri, M.G. (1998) The Maintenance of Treatment Effects in the Long-Term Management of Obesity. *Clinical Psychology: Science and Practice*, **5**, 4.

Perri, M. (2002) Improving Maintenance in Behavioural Treatment. In Fairburn, C.G. and Brownell, K.D. (eds) *Eating Disorders and Obesity: A comprehensive handbook*. 2nd edition. New York: The Guilford Press.

Pescatello, L.S. & VanHeest, J.L. (2000) Physical activity mediates a healthier body weight in the presence of obesity. *British Journal of Sports Medicine*, **34**, 86–93.

Pinaquy, S., Chabrol, H., Simon, C., Louvet, J.-P. & Barbe, P. (2003) Emotional Eating, Alexithymia and Binge Eating Disorder in Obese Women. *Obesity Research*, **11** (2), 195–201.

Polivy, J. & Herman, C.P. (1992) Undieting: A program to help people stop dieting. *International Journal of Eating Disorders*, **11**, 261–268.

Pomerleau, J., McKeigue, P.M. & Charturvedi, N. (1999) Factors associated with obesity in South Asian, Afro-Caribbean and European women. *International Journal of Obesity*, **23**, 25–33.

Popkess-Vawter, S., Brandau, C. & Straub, J. (1998) Triggers of overeating and related intervention strategies for women who weight cycle. *Applied Nursing Research*, **11** (2), 69–76.

Power, C. & Parsons, T. (2000) Nutritional & other influences in childhood as predictors of adult obesity. *Proceedings of the Nutrition Society*, **59**, 267–272.

Prior, V. & Glaser, D. (2006) *Understanding Attachment and Attachment Disorders*. London: Jessica Kingsley Publishers.

Prochaska, J.O. & DiClemente, C.C. (1984) *The transtheoretical approach: Crossing Traditional Boundaries of Therapy*. Homewood, Ill.: Dow Jones-Irwin.

Prochaska, J.O., DiClemente, C.C. & Norcross, J.C. (1992) In Search of How People Change. *Amercan Psychologist*, **47**, 1102–1114.

Prochaska, J.O., DiClemente, C.C., Velicer, W.F. & Rossi, J.S. (1993) Standardized, Individualized, Interactive and Personalized Self-help Programs for Smoking Cessation. *Health Psychology*, **12**, 399–405.

Pronk, N.P. & Wing, R.R. (1994) Physical Activity and Long-Term Maintenance of Weight Loss. *Obesity Research*, **2** (6), 587–99.

Puhl, R. & Brownell, K.D. (2002) Stigma, discrimination and obesity. In Fairburn, C.G. and Brownell, K.D. (eds) *Eating Disorders and Obesity: A comprehensive handbook*. 2nd edition. New York: Guilford Press.

Puska, P., Nissinen, A., Tuomilehto, J., Salonen, J.T., Koskela, K., McAlister, A., Kottke, T.E., Maccoby, N. & Farquar, J.W. (1985) The Community-Based Strategy to Prevent Coronary Heart Disease: Conclusions from the Ten Years of the North Karelia Project. *Annual Review of Public Health*, **6**, 147–193.

Rabinor, J.R. (2004) The Therapist's Voice. *Eating Disorders*, **12**, 257–261.

Råstam, M., Gillberg, C., Gillberg, I.C. & Johansson, M. (1997) Alexithymia in anorexia nervosa: a controlled study using the 20-item Toronto Alexithymia Scale. *Acta Psychiatrica Scandinavia*, **95**, 385–388.

Ratigan, B. & Aveline, M. (1988) Interpersonal group therapy. In Aveline, M. and Dryden, W. (eds) *Group Therapy in Britain*. Milton Keynes: OUP, 43–64.

Raynes, E., Auerbach, C. & Botyanski, N.C. (1989) Level of object representation and psychic structure deficit in obese persons. *Psychological Reports*, **64**, 291–294.

Renjilian, D.A. Perri, M.G. Nezu, A.M. McKelvey, W.F. Sherner, R.L. & Anton, S.D. (2001) Individual vs. group therapy for obesity: Effects of matching participants to their treatment preferences. *Journal of Consulting and Clinical Psychology*, **69** (4), 717–721.

Rennie, K.L. & Jebb, S.A. (2005) Prevalence of obesity in Great Britain. *Obesity Reviews*, **6**, 11–12.

Riding, R.J. & Rayner, S. (1998) *Cognitive styles and learning strategies: understanding style differences in learning and behaviour*. London: David Fulton.

Roberts, S.J. (1996). The sequelae of childhood sexual abuse: a primary care focus for adult female survivors. *Nurse Practitioner*, **21** (12 pt 1), 42, 45, 49–52.

Rogers, C. (1979) *On Becoming a Person: A Therapist's View of Psychotherapy*. London: Constable.

Rogers, C. (1981) *Client-Centered Therapy*. London: Constable.

Rookus, M.A., Burema, J. & Frijters, J.E. (1988) Changes in body mass index in young adults in relation to number of life events experienced. *International Journal of Obesity*, **12** (1), 29–39.

Rosmond, R. (2005) Role of stress in the pathogenesis of the metabolic syndrome. *Psychoneuroendocrinology*, **30**, 1–10.

Rössner, S. (1992) Factors determining the long-term outcome of obesity. In Björntorp, P. and Brodoff, B.N. (eds) *Obesity*. Philadelphia: J. B. Lippincott Company.

Rothblum, E.D. (1994) 'I'll die for the revolution but don't ask me not to diet': Feminism and the continuing stigmatisation of obesity. In Fallon, P., Katzman, M.A. and Wooley, S.C. (eds) *Feminist Perspectives on Eating Disorders*. New York: Guilford Press.

Rothman, A.J., Salovey, P., Turvey, C. & Fishkin, S.A. (1993) Attributions of Responsibility and Persuasion: Increasing Mammography Utilization Among Women Over 40 with an Internally Oriented Message. *Health Psychology*, **12**, 39–47.

Roughan, P., Seddon, E. & Vernon-Roberts, J. (1990) Long-Term Effects of a Psychologically Based Group Programme for Women Preoccupied with Body Weight and Eating Behaviour. *International Journal of Obesity*, **14**, 135–147.

Rowston, W.M., McCluskey, S.E., Gazet, J.C., Lacey, J.H., Franks, G. & Lynch, D. (1992) Eating Behaviour, Physical Symptoms and Psychological Factors Associated with Weight Reduction Following the Scopinaro Operation as Modified by Gazet. *Obesity Surgery*, **2** (4), 355–360.

Saris, W.H.M., Blair, S.N., van Baak, M.A., Eaton, S.B., Davies, P.S.W., Di Pietro, L., Fogelholm, M., Rissanen, A., Schoeller, D., Swinburn, B., Tremblay, A., Westerterp, K.R. & Wyatt. H. (2003) How much physical activity is enough to prevent unhealthy weight gain? Outcome of the IASO 1st Stock Conference and consensus statement. *Obesity Reviews*, **4** (2), 101.

Sarlio-Lahteekorva, S. (1998) Relapse stories in obesity. *The European Journal of Public Health*, **8** (3), 203–209.

Schmidt, U., Jiwany, A. & Treasure, J. (1993) A controlled study of alexithymia in eating disorders. *Comprehensive Psychiatry*, **34**, 54–58.

Schmidt, U. & Treasure, J. (1997) *getting better bit(e) by bit(e): a survival kit for sufferers of bulimia nervosa and binge eating disorder*. Hove: Psychology Press.

Schoeller, D.A., Shay, K. & Kushner, R.F. (1997) How much physical activity is needed to minimize weight gain in previously obese women. *American Journal of Clinical Nutrition*, **66**, 551–556.

Schoemaker, C., McKitterick, C.R., McEwen, B.S. & Kreek, M.J. (2002) Bulimia nervosa following psychological and multiple child abuse: support for the self-medication hypothesis in a population based cohort study. *International Journal of Eating Disorders*, **32**, 381–388.

Schore, A.N. (1997) A century after Freud's project: is a rapprochement between psychoanalysis and neurobiology at hand? *Journal of the American Psychoanalytic Association*, **45** (3), 807–40.

Schore, A.N. (1997a) Early organization of the nonlinear right brain and development of a predisposition to psychiatric disorders. *Developmental Psychopathology*, **9** (4), 595–631.

Schore, A.N. (1997b) Interdisciplinary developmental research as a source of clinical models. In Moskowitz, M., Monk, CC. and Ellman, S. (eds) *The Neurobiological and Developmental Basis of Psychotherapeutic Intervention*. Northvale, N.J.: Aronson, 1–71.

Schore, A.N. (2000) Attachment and the regulation of the right brain. *Attachment & Human Development*, **2** (1), 23–47.

Schore, A.N. (2001) Effects of a secure attachment relationship on right brain development, affect regulation, and infant mental health. *Infant Mental Health Journal*, **22** (1-22), 7–66.

Schore, A.N. (2002) Dysregulation of the right brain: a fundamental mechanism of traumatic attachment and the psychopathogenesis of post-traumatic stress disorder. *Australian and New Zealand Journal of Psychiatry*, **36**, 9–30.

Schore, A.N. (2003) *Affect Regulation and the Repair of Self*. New York: W.W. Norton & Co.

Schutz, W. (1979) *Profound Simplicity*. London: Turnstone Books.

Schwartz, M.B. & Brownell, K.D. (1995) Matching individuals to weight loss treatments: a survey of obesity experts. *Journal of Consulting and Clinical Psychology*, **63**, 149–153.

Schwarzer, R. & Fuchs, R. (1995) Changing risk behaviour and adopting health behaviours: The role of self-efficacy beliefs. In Bandura, A. (ed) *Self-efficacy in Changing Societies*. Cambridge, NY: Cambridge University Press.

Seamoore, D., Buckroyd, J., & Stott, D. (2006) Changes in eating behaviour following group therapy for women who binge eat: a pilot study. *Journal of Psychiatric and Mental Health Nursing*, **13**, 337–346.

Seidell, J.C. & Tijhuis, M.A.R. (2002) Obesity and Quality of Life. In Fairburn, C.G. and Brownell, K.D. (eds) *Eating Disorders and Obesity: A comprehensive handbook*. 2nd edition. New York: The Guilford Press.

Shaw, K., Del Mar, C., O'Rourke, P., Tito, F. Exercise for obesity. (Protocol) *The Cochrane Database of Systematic Reviews* 2002, Issue 3. Art. No: CD003817. pub2. DOI: 10.1002/14651858.CD003817.pub2.

Shaw, K., O'Rourke, P., Del Mar, C. & Kenardy, J. (2005) Psychological interventions for overweight or obesity. *The Cochrane Database of Systematic Reviews*, Issue 2. Art. No.: CD003818.pub2. DOI: 10.1002/14651858.CD003818.pub2.

Sickel, A.E., Noll, J.G., Moore, P.J., Putnam, F.W. & Trickett, P.K. (2002) The Long-term Physical Health and Healthcare Utilization of Women Who Were Sexually Abused as Children. *Journal of Health Psychology*, **7** (5), 583–597.

Siegel, A.M. (1996) *Heinz Kohut and the Psychology of the Self*. London: Routledge.

Sjöström, L., Rissanen, A., Andersen, T., Boldrin, M., Golay, A., Koppeschaar, H., & Krempf, M. (1998) Randomised placebo-controlled trial of orlistat for weight loss and prevention of weight regain in obese patients. *The Lancet*, **352** (9123), 167–172.

Smolak, L. & Murnen, S.K. (2002) A Meta-Analytic Examination of the Relationship Between Child Sexual Abuse and Eating Disorders. *International Journal of Eating Disorders*, **31**, 136–150.

Sroufe, L.A. (1995) *Emotional Development: The organization of emotional life in the early years*. Cambridge: Cambridge University Press.

Stein, M.B. & Barrett-Connor, E. (2000) Sexual assault and Physical Health: Findings From a Population-Based Study of Older Adults. *Psychosomatic Medicine*, **62**, 838–843.

Steptoe, A., Wardle, J., Lipsey, Z., Oliver, G., Pollard, T.M. & Davies, G.J. (1998) The effects of life stress on food choice. In Murcott, A. (ed) *The nation's diet: the social science of food choice*. Harlow, UK: Addison Wesley Longman Ltd.

Stern, D.N. (2000) *The Interpersonal World of the Infant*. New York: Basic Books.

Summers, F. (1994) *Object Relations Theories and Psychopathology: A Comprehansive Text*. NJ: Analytic Press.

Tanco, S., Linden, W. & Earle, T. (1998) Well-Being and Morbid Obesity in Women: A Controlled Therapy Evaluation. *International Journal of Eating Disorders*, **23**, 325–339.

Tasca, G.A., Ritchie, K., Conrad, G., Balfour, L., Gayton, J., Lybandon, V. & Bissada, H. (2006) Attachment scales predict outcome in a randomized controlled trial of two group therapies for binge eating disorder: An aptitude by treatment interaction. *Psychotherapy Research*, **16** (1), 106–121.

Telch, C.F. & Agras, W.S. (1996) Do emotional states influence binge eating in the obese? *International Journal of Eating Disorders*, **20**, 271–279.

Texeira, P.J., Going, S.B., Sardinha, L.B. & Lohman, T.G. (2005) A review of psychosocial pre-treatment predictors of weight control. *Obesity Reviews*, **6**, 43–65.

Thorne, B. (1988) The Person-Centred Approach to Large Groups. In Aveline, M. and Dryden, W. (eds) *Group Therapy in Britain*. Milton Keynes: OUP, 185–207.

Tinker, J.E. & Tucker, J.A. (1997) Environmental events surrounding natural recovery from obesity. *Addictive Behaviors*, **22**, 571–575.

Troisi, A., Massaroni, P. and Cuzzolaro, M. (2005) Early separation anxiety and adult attachment style in women with eating disorders. *British Journal of Clinical Psychology*, **44**, 89–97.

Trombini, E., Baldaro, B., Bertaccini, R., Mattei, C., Montebarocci, O. & Rossi, N. (2003) Maternal attitudes and attachment styles in mothers of obese children. *Perceptual and Motor Skills*, **97**, 613–620.

Tuckman, B.W., (1965) Developmental sequence in small groups. *Psychological Bulletin*, **63** (6), 384–389.

Tudor, L.E., Keemar, K., Tudor, K., Valentine, J. & Worrall, M. (2004) *The Person-Centred Approach: A Contemporary Introduction*. Basingstoke: Palgrave Macmillan.

Turner, S. & Lee, D. (1998) *Measures in Post Traumatic Stress Disorder: A Practitioner's Guide*. Windsor: NFER-Nelson.

Turner, S. & Moss, S. (1996) The health needs of adults with learning disabilities and the *Health of the Nation* strategy. *Journal of Intellectual Disability Research*, **40** (5), 438–450.

Van, Gaal, P.F., Rissanen, A.M., Scheen, A.J., Ziegler, O., Rössner, S. (2005) Effects of the cannabinoid-1 receptor blocker rimonobant on weight reduction and cardiovascular risk factors in overweight patients: 1-year experience from the RIO-Europe study. *The Lancet*, **365**, Issue 9468, 1389–1397.

Vila, G., Zinner, E., Dabbas, M., Bertrand, C., Robert, J.J., Ricour, C. & Mouren-Siméoni, M.C. (2004) Mental Disorders in Obese Children and Adolescents. *Psychosomatic Medicine*, **66**, 387–394.

Visvanathan, R. & Chapman, I. (2005) Older people should not be misinformed about being overweight. *British Medical Journal*, **331**, 20–27 August 2005, 452–3.

Vogele, C. & Florin, I. (1997) Psychophysiological responses to food exposure: an experimental study in binge eaters. *International Journal of eating Disorders*, **21** (2), 147–157.

Ward, A., Ramsay, R. & Treasure, J. (2000) Attachment Research in Eating Disorders. *British Journal of Medical Psychology*, **73**, 35–51.

Wardle, J., Waller, J. & Rapoport, L. (2001) Body dissatisfaction and binge eating in obese women: the role of restraint and depression. *Obesity Research*, **9**, 778–787.

Walfish, S. (2004) Self-Assessed Emotional Factors Contributing to Increased Weight Gain in Pre-surgical Bariatric Patients. *Obesity Surgery*, **14**, 1402–1405.

Weiss, E.L., Longhurst, J.G. & Mazure, C.M. (1999) Childhood Sexual Abuse as a Risk Factor for Depression in Women: Psychosocial and Neurobiological Correlates. *The American Journal of Psychiatry*, **156**, 816–828.

Weiderman, M.W., Sansone. R.A. & Sansone, L.A. (1999) Obesity among sexually abused women: an adaptive function for some? *Women and Health*, **29** (1), 89–100.

White, P.J. (2002) Big problem. *Communitycare*, **25** (31), 32–33.

WHO (1997) Obesity – prevention and management of the global epidemic. The WHO Consultation on Obesity, Geneva 3–5 June.

Will, M.J., Franzblau, E.B. & Kelley, A.E. (2003) Neucleus accumbens mu-opioids regulate intake of a high-fat diet via activation of a distributed brain network. *Journal of Neuroscience*, **23**, 2882–2888.

Will, M.J., Franzblau, E.B. & Kelley, A.E. (2004) The amygdala is critical for opioid-mediated binge eating of fat. *Neuroreport*, **15**, 1857–1860.

Williamson, D.F., Thompson, T.J., Anda, R.F., Dietz, W.H. & Felitti, V. (2002). Body weight and obesity in adults and self-reported abuse in childhood. *International Journal of Obesity*, **26**, 1075–1082.

Wilson, G.T. (1994) Behavioral treatment of obesity: Thirty years and counting. *Advances in Behavior Research and Therapy*, **16**, 35–75.

Wilson, T.G., Vitousek, K.M. & Loeb, K.L. (2000) Stepped Care Treatment for Eating Disorders. *Journal of Consulting and Clinical Psychology*, **68** (4), 564–572.

Wing, R.R. & Klem, M. (2002) Characteristics of Successful Weight Maintainers. In Fairburn, C.G. and Brownell, K.D. (eds) *Eating Disorders and Obesity*. New York: The Guilford Press.

Wing, R.R. & Jakicic, J.M. (2000) Changing Lifestyle: Moving From Sedentary to Active. In Bouchard, C. (ed) *Physical Activity and Obesity*. Champaign, IL.: Human Kinetics.

Winnicott, D.W. (1953) Transitional Objects and Transitional Phenomena: A Study of the First Not-Me Possession. *The International Journal of Psychoanalysis*, **34**, 89–97.

Wolf, A.M. (2002) The Health Economics of Obesity and Weight Loss. In Fairburn, C.G. and Brownell, K.D. (eds) *Eating Disorders and Obesity*. New York: The Guilford Press.

Wonderlich, S.A., Crosby, R.D., Mitchell, J.E., Thompson, K.M., Redlin, J., Demuth, G., Smyth, J. & Haseltine, B. (2001) Eating Disturbance and Sexual Trauma in Childhood and Adulthood. *International Journal of Eating Disorders*, **30**, 401–412.

Yalom, I.D. with Leszcz, M. (2005) *The Theory and Practice of Group Psychotherapy*. 5th edition. New York: Basic Books.

Yamanouchi, K., ShinozakiI, T., Chikada, K., Nishikawa, T., Ito, K., Shimizu, S., Ozawa, N., Suzuki, Y., Maeno, H. & Kato, K. (1995) Daily walking combined with diet therapy is a useful means for obese NIDDM patients not only to reduce body weight but also to inprove insulin sensitivity. *Diabetes Care* **18**, 775–778.

Yanovski, S.Z. (2003) Binge eating disorder and obesity in 2003: Could treating an eating disorder have a positive effect on the obesity epidemic? *International Journal of Eating Disorders*, **34**, S117–S120.

Yanovski, S.Z. (2003a) Sugar and Fat: Cravings and Aversions. *Journal of Nutrition*, **133**, 835S–837S.

Zdrodowski, D. (1996) Eating out: The experience of eating in public for the "overweight" woman. *Women's Studies International Forum*, **19** (6) 655–664.

Zimmerman, P. (1999) Structure and functions of internal working models of attachment and their role for emotion regulation. *Attachment and Human Development*, **1**, 291–306.

Zlotnick, C., Shea, T.M., Rosen, K., Simpson, E., Mulrenin, K., Begin, A. & Pearlstein, T. (1997) An Affect-Management Group for Women with Posttraumatic Stress Disorder and Histories of Childhood Sexual Abuse. *Journal of Traumatic Stress*, **10**, 425–436.

Index

absences 44, 46
abusive behaviour 45
acceptable goal 124
activity
    changing attitudes and behaviour 30–1
    group members' relationship with 135–6
    increasing 28–9
    physical benefits 29–30
    psychological benefits 30
activity audit 133–4
activity group 38
Addis, M.E. 42
Adult Attachment Interview 39
Adverse Childhood Experiences (ACE) xxi
affect management 19
Affect Management Skills Training 19
age, obesity and 41
Agras, W.S. xix, xxiii, 35
aims of treatment 15
Alexander, Patricia Nell 38
alexithymia 12, 16–17, 63
all or nothing thinking 8
anger 17, 26
anger avoidance xix
anorexia 33
anxiety
    attachment xx
    as group member 40
    obesity and xxii, 17
Armitage, C.J. 9
Arnow, B. 15, 16, 39
art therapy 22
attachment anxiety xx
attachment avoidance xx
attachment difficulties 35
attachment history xx
attachment theory 6
Aveline, M. 12, 38, 39, 43
Aversa, A. xx

Bandura, Albert 9, 11, 24, 99
Barbie doll 123
bariatric surgery xx, xxi
Barrett-Connor, E. xxii
Baumeister, R.F. xix

behavioural strategies xxiii
behavioural theory 3
beliefs about food 87–8
Benjamin, O. xix
Benson, J.F. 12, 13, 38, 47, 49
Bidgood, J. xxii, 5, 35
binge eating disorder (BED) xv, xix, xxiii,
    34–5, 36
    childhood maltreatment and xxi
    stress and xx
Binge Eating Scale 15, 16
black and white thinking 145
Blackburn, G.L. 15
Blair, S.N. 29
Bloom, C. 7
body acceptance 126
body appreciation 128
body esteem 23–4, 114, 154
    food choice and 121
body image 23, 24, 114
Body Mass Index (BMI) xxiv, 35, 39–40
Boersma, H. xxii, 35
boredom 17
boundary setting 44–6
Bowlby, J. 6
brainstorming 26, 62, 63–4, 117
breaks 46
Brodney, S. 29
Brownell, K.D. xvi, xxiii, 4, 12
Buckroyd, J. xxii, 5, 6, 18, 22, 25, 34, 35, 37
buddying 27, 69–70, 73–4, 79-80, 142
bulimia 33
Burgard, D. 7
Byrne, S.M. xvi, xx, 145

Canetti, L. xix
cardiovascular disease risk 30
Carrier, K.M. 23
Carryer, J. 4
catastrophising 8
Chagnon, Y.C. xviii
champion slimmers 36
change, theory of (Prochaska and DiClemente)
    9–10, 30
    see also Wheel of Change

Chapman, I. 41
childhood mealtime scenario 74–7
childhood sexual abuse (CSA) xxi, xxii
Chua, J.L. xix
Ciarrochi, J. 13
Ciechanowski, P. xx
Ciliska, D. 23
circle of support exercise 89–90
Clark, M. 42
Clerici, M. 16
Clinical Outcomes in Routine Evaluations (CORE)
    15, 16
Cochrane, C. 16
Cogan, J. xvi, 4, 23, 42
cognitive behavioural therapy (CBT) xv, xxiii,
    7–8, 87
Cognolato, S. 12
Colantuoni, C. xxii
Collins, P. xvi, xviii
Colvin, R.H. xvii, 11
comfort eating xvii, xviii, xx, xxii
commercial weight loss programmes 41
Commissioning Obesity Services 43
confidentiality 44
congruence 5
Connelly, J.C. 29
Conner, M. 9
consolidation 158
contact 27, 38, 45
Conway, B. xv, xvi
Cooper, Z. 8, 31
core conditions 5, 6
cortisol xx
Courcoulas, A.P. 40
Crisp, A.H. 4
cultural pressures 123

Dallman, M.F. xxii
Dana, M. 7
Davis, E. xxii
De Chouly De Lenclave, M.B. 16
de Zwaan, M. 16
Deaver, C.M. xix
depression xxi, 33
Despré, J.-P. xvi
Devlin, M.J. xv, 17
diabetes, Type 2 xx, 25, 31, 40
DiClemente, C.C. 9, 10, 39, 40
diet sheets 38
discrimination 4
dodo effect 3

Dokter, D. 22
Douketis, J.D. xv
Dryden, W. 12, 38, 43

eating behaviour, obese people's understanding
    of 35
Eberhardt, M.S. xx
Egolf, B. xviii
Eldredge, K.L. xxiii, 35
Elfhag, K. xxiii
Emotional Eating Scale 15, 16
emotional eating xx, xxiii, 35, 134
emotional intelligence, developing 16–18
emotional language 17
empathy 5
    failure of 49
    in group leaders 50
employee assistance programme 38
empowerment 24, 63
Encinosa, W.E. xvi
environment, family xxi
Epel, E. xx
equipment for group members 46–7
Ernsberger, P. xvi, 4, 23, 42
Evans, C. 15, 16
exclusion criteria 40–1
exercise *see* activity

Fabricatore, A.N. 4
Fairburn, C.G. 35
Fallon, P. 7
family
    attitudes to exercise 135
    dysfunction xxi
    feelings 67–8
    food and 136
fat and thin exercise 117–18
fears *see* hopes and fears
feelings 140
    family 67–8
    managing 64, 68, 71, 74, 80–1, 171–2
    names for 63–4
Felitti, V.J. xx, xxi, xxii, xxiii
feminist theory 6–7
Fichter, M.M. xvi, xix, 25, 35
Field, A.E. xv
Flores, P.J. xx
Florin, I. xix
food
    beliefs about 87–8
    family and 136

food and mood sheet 169
food choice 27–8, 103, 111–12, 113, 119,
    151–2
  body esteem and 121
  emotional meanings of 106
  goals 107–8
food diary 59
Food in the Family exercise 175
food planning sheets 71
Forbes, D. xviii
Foreyt, J.P. xix, 23, 35
Foster, G.D. xvi
Freeman, L.M. xix, xx
Freud, Sigmund 5
Friedman, M.A. 4
Frothingham, T.E. xxi
Fuchs, R. 11

Garland, J. 12
Garner, D.M. xv, xvi, 4, 23, 27
Geliebter, A. xx
genetic inheritance xviii
George, C. 39
Gerhardt, S. 18
Gil, K.M. xix, xx
Gilbert, S. 39
Glaser, D. xx
Glenny, A. xv
Gluck, M.E. xix, xx, 35
goals, reasonable, setting 124
Goleman, Daniel 16
Goodrick, G.K. xix, 11, 23, 35
Goodspeed-Grant, P. xxii, 35
Goran, M.I. 30
Gormally, J. 11, 15, 16, 39
Grilo, C.M. xxi
grounding 74
group confidentiality statement 163
group development 25–6
group discussion 26
group leader 13
  empathy and 23
  men as 50
  Rogerian model 46
  role of 25
group letters 156, 157
group psychotherapy for bulimia nervosa 12
groups, value of 9, 11–13
Guided Fantasy 119–20, 179
guilt 17
Gustafson, T.B xxi

Hampson, S.E. 42
Hardman, A.E. 31
Harrison, K.R. 23
Hartford, M.E. 12
Harvey, E.L. xvi, 4, 5
Haslam, D.W. xv, xvi
Hay, P.J. xxiii
Hayaki, J. 12
Hayward, L.M. xix, 25
Heatherton, T.F. xix
Heenan, C. 7
Heiat, A. 41
Heinrichs, M. xx
Herman, C.P. 7, 23
Herman, J.L. 19
Hodge, J. 47
Holmes, J. 6
home-based activities 31
hope in relationships 23, 25
    see also hopes and fears
hopes and fears 47, 53–5, 64,
    153–4
Hoppe, R. 49
Houston, G. 3, 5
Howe, D. 6
Hulme, P.A. xxii
Hunter, J. xx
Hyde, K. 38, 46

imprisonment, family xxi
inclusion criteria 39–40
information sharing 55
inter-personal therapy (IPT) xv
introductory exercise 53

Jacob 63
Jakicic, J.M. 28, 30, 31
James, O. xviii
James, P.T. xvi
James, W.P.T. xv, xvi
Jebb, S.A. xv, 41
Jeffery, R.W. xvi, xvii, xxiii, 11, 25
Jia, H. xxi

Kahn, M. 6
Kamin-Shaaltiel, S. xix
Kasila, K. 10
Kasser, T. xviii
Kenardy, J. xix
Kendall, P.C. xvi
Kendall-Tackett, K. xxii

Kent, A. xxi
Kern, L.S. 34
King, A.C. 29
King, T.K. xxii
Klem, M.L. xvi, 29
Kohut, Heinz 6, 59
Kopp, W. xxi

lateness 44, 45
Latner, J.D. 27
Lawrence, M. 7
Lean, M.E.J. 31
learning disabled people 40
learning group 38
learning styles 3
Leather, S. xviii
Lee, D. 39
Lee, L. 4
length of intervention 42–3
Leserman, J. xxii
Lessem, P.A. 6
Levine, A.S. xxii
Lewis, V.J. 11, 23
Liebbrand, R. xvi, 25
lifestyle exercises 29, 31
Linde, J.A. xix
Lissau, I. xxi
listening skills 46, 47, 55
Logue, A.W. xvii, xviii, xix
Logue, E. 10
Loneck, B. 38
loneliness xxii
loss xxi
Lowe, M.R. xxii
Lyons, M.A. xxii, 35
Lyons, P. 7

MacMillan, H.L. xxii
Mahalik, J.R. 42
Maiese, D.R. 29
Manson, J.E. 31
Marcus, M.D. xix, 35
Masheb, R.M. xxi
mastery experiences 11
Matsakis, A. 19
Maunder, R. xx
McElroy, M. xviii, 7
McFarlane, T. 23
McKisack, C. 12, 39, 50
meal patterns xxiii
meal planning 70–1, 80, 173

meeting room, location and layout 43
men
    as group leaders 50
    obesity programme treatment for 42
    self-esteem and 42
mental illness xxi
menus, making 102
Miller, W.C. 28, 30
Mills, J.K. xxi
Mitchell, J.E. 40
Möller-Leimkühler, A.M. 42
Mollon, P. 6, 19
monitoring sheet 59–60
    compliance 62
Morris, J.N. 31
Morrison, A.L. 23
mortality risk, activity and 29
Moss, S. 40
mothers 81, 83–5, 88
    nurturing and 143–4
    patchwork mother exercise 90
motivation 65–7, 145–6
motivational enhancement 58–9
motivational wheel see Wheel of Change
Murnen, S.K. xxi

negative feelings 17
neglect xxi

objectives of treatment 16
O'Brien, M.O. 3, 5
Ogden, J. xvii, xix, 9, 49
Olson, S.B. xvii, 11
Omaha, J. 19
O'Meara, S. xv, xvi
Omichinski, L. 23
opioid system xxii
Orbach, S. 7, 119
Orford, J. xviii
Orlistat xvi, 41
overeating, management of 62–3
overview 97–9, 129–31, 155–6, 177, 181–5
oxytocin xx

Parsons, T. xviii, xxi
patchwork mother exercise 90
Pendleton, V.R. 27
Perri, M. xvi, 25, 27, 31, 42
person centred theory (Rogers) 3, 4–5, 6
Pescatello, L.S. 29
physical abuse xxi

physicality, vision of 141
Pinaquy, S. 16, 17
Polivy, J. 7, 23
Pomerleau, J. 40
Popkess-Vawter, S. xix
population study 35
positive (self)-talk 127–8
post traumatic stress disorders xx, 50
Power, C. xxi
power/control xix
pregnancy 41
prejudice 4–5, 35
Prior, V. xx
problem solving 105–6
process of change diagram 58–9, 167
Prochaska, J.O. 9, 10, 39, 40, 58
programme outline 165
progress and development, review of 155–6
Pronk, N.P. xvi, 29
psychoanalytical model of group leadership 46
psychodynamic theory 3, 5, 47
psychological welfare 23
psychotherapy xxiii
Puhl, R. 4
purpose of group 44
Puska, P. 11

Rabinor, J.R. 25
Rastâm, M. 16
rates of obesity xv, xvi
Ratigan, B. 39
Rayner, S. 3
Raynes, E. xx
recruitment of group members 37–8
referral 37–8
relapse 9
relationships 142, 149–50
  developing 24–7
Rene, A. xv, xvi
Renjilian, D.A. 12
Rennie, K.L. xv, 41
responsibility xvii, 10
Riding, R.J. 3
Rimonabant xvi
Roberts, S.J. xxii
Rogers, Carl 4–5, 6
Rookus, M.A. xix
Rosmond, R. xx
Rössner, S. xxiii
Rothblum, E.D. 4
Rother, S. 37

Rothman, A.J. 10
Roughan, P. 23
Rowston, W.M. xxi

Saris, W.H.M. 30
Sarlio-Lahteenkorva, S. xxii
Sarwer, D.B. xxi
Schmidt, U. 16, 58
Schoeller, D.A. 30
Schoemaker, C. xx
Schore, A.N. xx, 4
Schutz, W. 12
Schwartz, M.B. xvi, xxiii
Schwarzer, R. 11
Scott, G. 13
Seamoore, D. 34
Seidell, J.C. 15
self, sense of 6
self-assertion 23
self-efficacy, theory of 9, 11, 23, 99
self-esteem 23, 33
  men and 42
self-hatred 114
self-help groups 27
self-nurture 18–24
self-referral 37, 39
sexual abuse xxi
  childhood (CSA) xxi, xxii
  of women xxii
Shapiro, C.M. 4
Shaw, K. xxiii, 8, 29, 30
shopping exercise 108
Sibutramine xvi
Sickel, A.E. xxi
Siegel, A.M. 6
size and shape, cultural messages about 123
size of group 38–9
slimmers, champion 36
Sjöström, L. xvi
smoking cessation 10
Smolak, L. xxi
social modelling 11
social persuasion 11
socio-economic status xviii, xxiii
solution focused therapy 63
Sotrensen, T.I.A. xxi
Sroufe, L.A. 6
Stein, M.B. xxii
stepometers 28, 31, 139–40, 141, 143
Steptoe, A. xix, 25
Stern, D.N. 6

stigmatisation 5, 35
stress xix–xx, xxii
subgroups of obese women xxiii
substance abuse xxi
suicidal xxi
Summers, F. 6
swimming 31

Tanco, S. 23
Tasca, G.A. xx
Telch, C.F. xix, xxiii, 35
Texeira, P.J. xvii
Thorne, B. 46
Tijhuis, M.A.R. 15
Tinker, J.E. 11
training of group leaders 49–50
transitional object 47
trauma xxi, 18–19, 35, 64, 74
Trauma Interview Schedule 39
Treasure, J. 58
Troisi, A. xx
Trombini, E. xx
trust 23, 25, 93–4, 142, 147–8
  exercise 94
Tucker, J.A. 11
Tuckman, B.W. 12
Tudor, L.E. 5
Turner, S. 39, 40

unconditional positive regard 5

value system 118
Van Gaal, P.F. xvi
VanHeest, J.L. 29
verbal abuse xxi
Vila, G. xx
violent behaviour xxi, 45

Visvanathan, R. 41
Vogele, C. xix

Wadden, T.A. xvi, xxiii, 4
Walfish, S. xx
walking 31
Waller, G. 12, 39, 50
Ward, A. xx
Wardle, J. 23
weight loss exercise 125–6
weight loss programmes 24–5
weight loss, sustained xv–xvi,
  xxiii–xxiv, 27
weightline/lifeline exercise 57–8
Weiss, E.L. xxii
Wheel of Change 10, 103, 145–6, 167
White, P.J. 5
Wiederman xxii
Will, M.J. xxii
Williams, G. xvi, xviii
Williamson, D.F. xxi
Wilson, G.T. xvi
Wilson, T.G. xv
Wing, R.R. xvi, xix, 28, 29, 30,
  31, 35
Winnicott, D.M. 47
Wolf, A.M. xv
Wonderlich, S.A. xxi
Wooley, S.C. xv, xvi, 4, 23, 27

Yalom, I.D. 8, 12, 44, 47
Yamanouchi, K. 31
Yanovski, S. xix, xxii

Zdrodowski, D. 4
Zimmerman, P. xx
Zlotnick, C. 19